ALL ABOUT THE SECOND COMING OF CHRIST

"10 Lessons to Understand
the Greatest Event in the
History of the World"

DR. NEALE B. OLIVER

WESTBOW
PRESS®
A DIVISION OF THOMAS NELSON
& ZONDERVAN

This book is a work of non-fiction. Unless otherwise noted, the author and the publisher make no explicit guarantees as to the accuracy of the information contained in this book and in some cases, names of people and places have been altered to protect their privacy.

WestBow Press books may be ordered through booksellers or by contacting:

WestBow Press
A Division of Thomas Nelson & Zondervan
1663 Liberty Drive
Bloomington, IN 47403
www.westbowpress.com
1 (866) 928-1240

Because of the dynamic nature of the Internet, any web addresses or links contained in this book may have changed since publication and may no longer be valid. The views expressed in this work are solely those of the author and do not necessarily reflect the views of the publisher, and the publisher hereby disclaims any responsibility for them.

Any people depicted in stock imagery provided by Getty Images are models, and such images are being used for illustrative purposes only. Certain stock imagery © Getty Images.

ISBN: 978-1-9736-5804-7 (sc)
ISBN: 978-1-9736-5805-4 (hc)
ISBN: 978-1-9736-5826-9 (e)

Library of Congress Control Number: 2019903584

Print information available on the last page.

WestBow Press rev. date: 01/20/2020

ENDORSEMENTS

Pastor Neale has written a must-read book for anyone wanting to make sense of the Second Coming of Christ. He writes in a simplistic way for all (believers and non-believers) to understand.

Darla Hamilton, Retired Teacher, Ft. Worth ISD

Pastor Neale Oliver has done a masterful job of breaking down the mystery surrounding the Second Coming of Christ and presenting it in a way anyone can understand. If you want to know more about Jesus' return, the book you are holding is a good place to start! Engaging and informative, All About The Second Coming Of Christ will help you better understand the greatest event in the history of the world and give you new insight in how to live your life with meaning and purpose today!

Scott Whitson, Executive Director, Southwest Metroplex Baptist Association

I could not put this book down. It is easy to read, but you will want to read it slowly so you can take in the wisdom and insight of each line. It is not what you think it is...it's so much more! I learned so much about the many verses I read, more than I thought a book could teach. Dr. Neale Oliver's style is warm and engaging, and how he delivered this message of the

Second Coming of Christ was genius. I have almost every page highlighted. It's a great, great book!

Power For Life Ministry President, Jerod Rost

I have over 3000 titles in my personal library, probably 10-20 concerning themselves with some facet of Biblical Revelation. This is the first book I have read that is orderly, organized, and succinct. It is not necessarily short; in fact, it is comprehensive, but so well written that it seems shorter than most. I have read all the different angles, thoughts, and "...isms" accepted today, and maybe it is because I lean this way in my own theological understanding, but I say, "Good job, Neale!" Or maybe it's because I am well read that I feel yours is the best one presented between the two covers. I've read much about the subject, and you treated it vigorously, simply, and exhaustively, and most importantly Biblically.

Charles Garrett, Exec. Dir.,
The Christian Heritage Foundation
Cleburne, Texas

A user-friendly primer that clearly explains biblical prophecy in a manner that facilitates both individual spiritual growth as well as a ministry of small group or one-on-one disciple development.

Rev. John Kanter, Messianic Jew
Ministry Representative Sojourner Ministries

I loved getting a chance to read and learn! This is going to make a difference in the lives of so many. So glad your dream of publishing this has come to fruition! #proud.

Ashton Oliver, Teacher and Daughter-in-law

DEDICATION:

*To my wife and best friend, Glynis. In the journey
of marriage and ministry, you have never wavered
in our call to serve the Lord and His church.
You are the best part of us. You are my forever always.*

CONTENTS

ACKNOWLEDGMENTS

This book is proof God can use anyone. It is through His grace and goodness, certainly not my very limited abilities, that you are holding this book.

My greatest thanks to the people of Henderson Street Baptist Church in Cleburne, Texas. You took a chance on a discouraged and wounded pastor and restored my faith in God's people and in God's church. You are the most encouraging people I have ever had the pleasure of serving. I will be forever in your debt the rest of my life.

Also, my thanks to the people of First Baptist Church in Whitewright, Texas, who for nine years patiently let me learn what it means to be a pastor. You were the first to receive the teaching of this book through a series of Sunday night Bible Studies. Your initial feedback planted the idea that one day a book could be possible. One day took twenty years.

To James Claborn, my first prayer partner as a pastor. I cannot put into words the encouragement you were to me in those early days as a pastor. Your feedback to the first teaching of the book encouraged me to keep teaching Jesus' Second Coming.

To Jason Summers, who kept telling me, "Preach the Word!" This book is directly from the Word.

To Norman Travis, who is at home with Jesus today. I love you in the Lord and cannot think about eternity without thinking of you. I look forward to serving in Jesus' eternal kingdom with you.

To Charlie and Doris Whitworth, who traveled 2.5 hours every Sunday for twelve weeks to listen to me preach the sermon series to this book. I owe you gas money.

To all the ministers I have had the pleasure to serve the Lord with, either as a youth minister or as a pastor. I hope in some way I have impacted your ministry in some positive way. I know you have impacted mine.

To my volunteer editors, Glynis, Robbi, Ashton, Darla, Kathleen, and Ray. Your help with the manuscript was completely necessary, and your honest evaluation was extremely helpful.

To Sarah Beth Boss the general editor, you are a gift from God, thank you for editing the book. I look forward to working together in future projects.

To Toby K. Easley of Feder Ink Publishing for copyediting the book and fine-tuning the final copy for print. Thank you and I look forward to working with you in the future.

To my parents, Roger and Lil, who brought me into this world. You encouraged me to spread my wings and soar like an eagle. This book would not be possible without you, obviously!

To my children Roger, Ryne, and Robbi, who have been the best PK's a father could ask for. You have never been a minute's trouble to your family; to the churches we've served, or to the communities we've lived. For that I say, "Thank you!" I am proud of the Christian adults you have become. I look forward to living in the New Jerusalem next door to you.

Finally, to those who would choose to criticize me for the content in the book. There are many different views of the Second Coming. I firmly believe everything in this book. If you don't, I would encourage you to write your book. The process will bless your life, as it has mine.

PREFACE: ABOUT THIS BOOK

The Second Coming of Christ is fact and is a culmination of thousands of years of Bible prophecies from the Old Testament to the New Testament. Jesus' return reveals the future of the Jews, the Gentiles, and the Christian Church. His return also reveals the eternity of both the saved and the lost.

All About The Second Coming of Christ is a book that comes from over 20 years of research, study, and teaching about the greatest event in the history of the world. Pastor Neale takes you on a journey to help you understand what the Bible teaches about the events surrounding Christ's return. Included at the end of the book is a glossary of Second Coming terms, and a group discussion guide that can be used in a large group, small group, or a one-on-one setting.

All About The Second Coming of Christ is not a seminary textbook. Each chapter is tailored for the person sitting in the church pew who desires to know what the Bible teaches about the Second Coming of Christ. When you finish reading this book you will have a good understanding of the events of Christ's return as they unfold through the pages of the Bible.

This book is written to alert the world that Jesus is coming again, and it could happen today!

INTRODUCTION

Welcome to what I hope and pray will become one of the favorite books in your library. If you're like me, studying the Second Coming of Christ is both fascinating and exciting. But it can also be intimidating and overwhelming. I hope this book will solve that problem for you. My goal is that what you read in the ten chapters of this book will give you a grasp of what I believe is the greatest event in the history of the world. I don't claim to be an expert by any means, but I have figured out a few things from the Bible as I have studied the Second Coming for over twenty years, and I want to share with you the great things I have discovered.

If you've never studied the events of the Second Coming, then this book is for you. This book is not a theological textbook for a seminary classroom, but is intended for the average person sitting in the church pew who desires to know the basics about Jesus and His return.

I suggest that you read this book three times. The first time just read it as if you were reading a novel. Don't make any notes in the margins or highlight any sentences or paragraphs, simply read for sheer information. The second time you read it underline, highlight, and write in the margin of the pages the things you want to remember. Review the seven points at the end of each chapter and answer the five questions. Finally, read the book a third time and soak in all the information—the notes in the margins, the highlighted parts in each chapter, the review points and the questions—just "let it all sink in." Let each event roll over in your mind. Think about the chronological order of each event, starting with the Rapture and ending with eternity in the New Heaven on the New Earth living in the New Jerusalem.

It's important that I tell you up front that my theological belief of the Second Coming is Dispensationalist. I believe in a Pre-Tribulation Rapture of the Church and I believe in a Pre-Millennial Second Coming. If you don't understand what that means right now, don't worry; you will by the end of the book. Dispensationalism has three main beliefs:

- God will keep His promises to both Israel and the church. God has a separate plan for both, and the church has not replaced Israel as God's people or in God's plan.
- We should read and interpret the Bible in the most plain, ordinary, normal manner, and as literally as possible.
- God does all things to reveal His glory to His creation.

Here is a list of pastors, scholars, and theologians who preach/teach the Dispensationalist view of the Bible:

- **Dr. W.A. Criswell**, Late Pastor of FBC Dallas for 46 years from 1944 to 1990.
- **Dr. Tony Evans**, Pastor of Oak Cliff Bible Church, Dallas, TX.
- **Dr. Billy Graham**, Considered by many to be the greatest modern-day world evangelist.
- **Dr. Tim LaHaye**, Author of the *Left Behind* book series.

- **Dr. John MacArthur,** Pastor of Grace Community Church, Sun Valley, CA, President of Master's University & Seminary, author of over 150 books, including *The MacArthur Study Bible.*
- **Dr. Dwight L. Moody,** Preacher and Evangelist. President of Chicago Bible Institute, later known as Moody Bible Institute.
- **Dr. J. Dwight Pentecost,** Professor of Bible Exposition Emeritus at Dallas Theological Seminary until his death.
- **Dr. Charles C. Ryrie**, Professor & Dean of doctoral studies at Dallas Theological Seminary, Editor of The Ryrie Study Bible. He is considered one of the most influential theologians of the 20th century.
- **Dr. Charles Stanley,** Pastor of First Baptist Church of Atlanta, GA, since 1971.
- **Dr. Chuck Swindoll,** Pastor of Stonebriar Community Church, Frisco, TX, and serves as Chancellor of Dallas Theological Seminary.
- **Dr. R.A. Torrey,** Pastor and Evangelist, Dean of Bible Institute of Los Angeles in 1912 (now Biola University). He is the author of over 40 books.
- **Dr. John Walvoord,** President of Dallas Theological Seminary 1952-1986; Author of over 30 books primarily focusing on eschatology and theology, including the book *The Rapture Question.*

It's important that you do not see the Second Coming as one single event, but see it as a series of events. Think of it as 4 phases: Phase 1: The Rapture; Phase 2: The Second Coming; Phase 3: The Millennial Kingdom; Phase 4: Eternity. Or, as a Two Act Play with an Intermission: Act 1: The Rapture; Intermission: The Tribulation; Act 2: The Second Coming.

In this book we will cover ten main events of the Second Coming: The Rapture, The New Heavenly Body, The Judgment Seat of Christ, A Marriage Made for Heaven, The Tribulation Period, The Second Coming of Christ, The Millennial Reign of Christ on the Earth, Satan's Last Stand, The Great White Throne Judgment, and Eternity in Heaven.

If you have been with me as I have taught this series in the churches I've pastored, I want you to know up front that some of my beliefs have evolved as I have studied and become more acquainted with God's Word. While these changes are minor in detail, my beliefs in the Dispensational view of the Second Coming have only become stronger. I always mention in the first session I teach that, while I believe everything in each lesson is Biblically accurate, I reserve the right to change my mind. I make that same claim to you, the reader of this book. However, in 20 years the only change in my teaching of the Second Coming from the first time I taught on it at First Baptist Church of Whitewright, Texas in 1998, to the most recent time I taught on it at Henderson Street Baptist Church in Cleburne, Texas in 2018, is in the eternal position of the New Jerusalem.

As you read this book you may become overwhelmed, but if you stick with it all the way to the end, I believe you will see the pieces of the puzzle come together, and by the conclusion of this book you will see a clear picture of Jesus and His Second Coming.

I have taken the opportunity to capitalize Earth, Heaven, Hell, and the Lake of Fire. It is my belief that these are real places just like New York, Los Angeles, London, and Tokyo. I have also capitalized Satan, Devil, anti-Christ, Beast, and False Prophet because they are the unholy trinity, just as God, Jesus, and the Holy Spirit are recognized by Christians as the Holy Trinity.

Let me close with this story: I was in my first pastorate at First Baptist Church of Whitewright, Texas, when at a Sunday night service, I mentioned the Great White Throne Judgment. A day or two later a member of the church knocked on the door of the parsonage across the street from the church to inform me that my reference to the Great White Throne Judgment was in error. Then he proceeded to correct my timing of the judgment. I remember listening intently as this man laid out the judgment of the world and where I had gone wrong. It was at that point and on that day that I made it my mission to never step into the pulpit or the front of the classroom unless I had put in the time to study, research, and support with Scripture what I was teaching and preaching. What you will read in the following pages is to the best of my ability studied, researched, and supported by Scripture. I firmly believe that this is the way the events of the Second Coming will unfold in chronological order.

I want to thank my friend for taking the time to educate a young and inexperienced preacher on the importance of getting it right every time. My friend left FBC Whitewright not long after that, and I hope it wasn't because he lost faith in me. What I do know is that God used him in my life to teach me a very important lesson. What you read and study in this book is partially the result of a conversation between a young pastor and a member of his church.

So, sit back, grab a hot cup of coffee (or in my case a hot cup of tea) and learn ALL ABOUT THE SECOND COMING OF CHRIST, the greatest event in the history of the world.

Until He Comes,
Dr. Neale B. Oliver

CHAPTER 1

THE RAPTURE

"We're not completely happy here because
we're not supposed to be here!
Earth is not our final home. We were created
for something much better."[1]
Rick Warren, *The Purpose Driven Life*

On April 3, 1843 all over the Northeast, half a million Adventists, disciples of evangelist William Miller, waited for the end of the world. Some disciples were on mountaintops, hoping to get a head start to Heaven. Others were in graveyards, planning to be raptured with their dearly departed loved ones. Some rich high society ladies joined together outside town so as not to enter God's kingdom with the common folk. When April 4th came and went with the world still intact, the followers of Miller were disillusioned, but they did not lose heart, for Miller had predicted several dates for the end of the world, but those dates also came and went.[2]

People have been trying to predict Jesus' return since He left. But the Bible is very clear that only God the Father knows when Jesus will return (Matthew 24:36). You'll never catch me predicting a date, but that doesn't mean I don't believe in a physical return of Jesus. I absolutely do. In fact, I believe the Rapture of the church is the next event on God's prophetic calendar.

You will not find the word "Rapture" in the Bible. Furthermore, neither will you find the word "Trinity." We, as Christians, do not question that God is Father, Son, and Holy Spirit. And neither should we question that Jesus will return for the church.

WHAT IS THE RAPTURE?

It is the next event on God's prophetic calendar. It is when Jesus leaves the right hand of God in Heaven and returns to the Earth to call believers up to meet Him in the clouds. The Rapture is NOT the Second Coming in terms of Christ coming to earth. At the Rapture Jesus descends to a point above the Earth. At the Second Coming Jesus descends to the Earth. At the Rapture, Jesus comes for the church. At the Second Coming Jesus comes with the church. The two events are separated by seven years (the Tribulation Period).

The Rapture is the disappearance of all true believing Christians from the Earth. It happens instantly, in the blink of an eye (1 Corinthians 15:52). Those who have died as believers will be resurrected first, and those believers who are alive will be resurrected second. All will meet Jesus in the sky (1 Thessalonians 4:16-17).

IS THE RAPTURE BIBLICAL?

That's the question in the church world today. Some question whether there is an actual Rapture of believers? I don't! I believe the Bible is crystal clear that Jesus will return before the Tribulation Period and take believers back to Heaven. Some believe the Rapture occurs in the middle of the Tribulation Period. Again, I don't. I believe it is pre-Tribulation. Let me show you why.

The concept of the Rapture is clearly taught in the Bible. The word "Rapture" comes from the Latin word "rapturo" which means to be "caught up." It is described in two passages—1 Corinthians 15:50-54, which focuses on the instantaneous change of believers, and 1 Thessalonians 4:13-18, which focuses on the resurrection of believers, both dead and alive.

> *1 **Corinthians** 15:50-54: Brothers, I tell you this: flesh and blood cannot inherit the kingdom of God, and corruption cannot inherit incorruption. Listen! I am telling you a mystery: We will not all fall asleep, but we will all be changed, in a moment, in the twinkling of an eye, at the last trumpet. For the trumpet will sound, and the dead will be raised incorruptible, and we will be changed. Because this corruptible must be clothed with incorruptibility, and this mortal must be clothed with immortality. Now when this corruptible is clothed with incorruptibility, and this mortal is clothed with immortality, then*

the saying that is written will take place: Death has been swallowed up in victory.

1 Thessalonians 4:13-18: We do not want you to be uninformed, brothers, concerning those who are asleep, so that you will not grieve like the rest, who have no hope. Since we believe that Jesus died and rose again, in the same way God will bring with Him those who have fallen asleep through Jesus. For we say this to you by a revelation from the Lord: We who are still alive at the Lord's coming will certainly have no advantage over those who have fallen asleep. For the Lord Himself will descend from heaven with a shout, with the archangel's voice, and with the trumpet of God, and the dead in Christ will rise first. Then we who are still alive will be caught up together with them in the clouds to meet the Lord in the air; and so we will always be with the Lord. Therefore encourage one another with these words.

It's obvious from these two passages that Paul believed in the Second Coming of Jesus and believed in the Rapture of the church. But also notice that Paul's teachings agree with Jesus' teachings:

John 5:24-29: I assure you: Anyone who hears My word and believes Him who sent Me has eternal life and will not come under judgment but has passed from death to life. I assure you: An hour is coming, and is now here, when the dead will hear the voice of the Son of God, and

4

those who hear will live. For just as the Father has life in Himself, so also He has granted to the Son to have life in Himself. And He has granted Him the right to pass judgment, because He is the Son of Man. Do not be amazed at this, because a time is coming when all who are in the graves will hear His voice and come out—those who have done good things, to the resurrection of life, but those who have done wicked things, to the resurrection of judgment.

John 11:21-27: *Then Martha said to Jesus, "Lord, if You had been here, my brother wouldn't have died. Yet even now I know that whatever You ask from God, God will give You." "Your brother will rise again," Jesus told her. Martha said, "I know that he will rise again in the resurrection at the last day." Jesus said to her, "I am the resurrection and the life. The one who believes in Me, even if he dies, will live. Everyone who lives and believes in Me will never die—ever. Do you believe this?" "Yes, Lord," she told Him, "I believe You are the Messiah, the Son of God, who was to come into the world."*

John 14:1-6: *"Your heart must not be troubled. Believe in God; believe also in Me. In My Father's house are many dwelling places; if not, I would have told you. I am going away to prepare a place for you. If I go away and prepare a place for you, I will come back and receive you to Myself, so that where I am you may be also.*

*You know the way where I am going." "Lord,"
Thomas said, "we don't know where You're
going. How can we know the way?" Jesus told
him, "I am the way, the truth, and the life. No
one comes to the Father except through Me."*

In John 5:29 Jesus mentions two resurrections. Those
that have done good will be resurrected to life. This is
the Rapture. Those who have done wicked things will be
resurrected to judgment. We will cover this in chapter nine,
The Great White Throne Judgment.

When Christ returns at the Rapture, He will call to Him
only those who are saved, the dead in Christ first, then those
who are alive second. This is called the "first resurrection"
(see Revelation 20:5) or the "resurrection of life" (John
5:29a). 1 Thessalonians 4:13-18 gives us 5 truths about the
Rapture:

1. According to Paul, *"those who have fallen asleep"* (v.
   14) are Thessalonian believers who died after Jesus'
   resurrection and before His return at the Second
   Coming. "Sleep" is metaphor for death.

2. Paul wrote this passage because the Thessalonian
   believers who were alive feared that *"those"* fellow
   believers who had died would miss the resurrection
   (Rapture). Paul assures them that is not the case in
   verses 15-18.

3. If *"those"* in verse 14 are coming with Jesus at the
   Second Coming, then they must already be with
   Him. How did they get to be with Him? The first

resurrection, which is the Rapture (see: Revelation 20:5-6).

4. This is not Paul's opinion, but it is a direct revelation of God (v. 15). Paul is giving the Thessalonians and us a brand-new teaching from God never mentioned before in the Bible.

5. Paul told the Thessalonians to encourage each other with these words.

For me this is proof that the Rapture of believers from the Earth is Biblical. It's an absolute fact! Jesus believed it, and Paul backed Him up, and that's good enough for me.

IS THE RAPTURE PRE-TRIBULATION?

Yes, I believe it will be. The Tribulation Period is the seven years between the Rapture and the Second Coming when Satan, the anti-Christ, and the False Prophet rule the world. There are three primary views of the Rapture:

1. Pre-Tribulation View: The Rapture will occur before the Tribulation Period.
2. Mid-Tribulation View: The Rapture will occur in the middle of the Tribulation Period.
3. Post-Tribulation View: The Rapture will occur after the Tribulation Period.

Let me give you six reasons I believe the Rapture is Pre-Tribulation:

1. The saved are not subject to the wrath of God. We have been saved by grace, and because of that we are exempt from the wrath of God that will be poured out on the Earth during the Tribulation Period. There are two primary purposes for the Tribulation Period. First, to give Israel one last chance to acknowledge and accept Jesus as Messiah. Second, to judge all the evil, wickedness, and sin on the Earth. God does this during the Tribulation Period.

   Daniel 12:1: At that time Michael the great prince who stands watch over your people will rise up. There will be a time of distress such as never has occurred since nations came into being until that time. But at that time all your people who are found written in the book will escape.

   Romans 5:9-10: ...Since we have now been declared righteous by His blood, we will be saved through Him from wrath. For if, while we were enemies, we were reconciled to God through the death of His Son, then how much more, having been reconciled, will we be saved by His life!

   1 Thessalonians 1:10: ...And to wait for His Son from heaven, whom He raised from the dead— Jesus, who rescues us from the coming wrath.

   1 Thessalonians 5:9: For God did not appoint us to wrath, but to obtain salvation through our Lord Jesus Christ...

Revelation 3:10: Because you have kept My command to endure, I will also keep you from the hour of testing (another name for the Tribulation Period) that is going to come over the whole world to test those who live on the earth.

All these verses talk about escaping, being saved, or being rescued from the coming wrath, which we know as the Tribulation Period.

2. In 1 Timothy 2:1-4, Christians are instructed to pray for the government and those in authority over it, and in Romans 13:1 we are told to subject ourselves to the governing authorities. But in Revelation John is very clear that Satan will control a worldwide government during the Tribulation Period, and the anti-Christ will come to power at the beginning of the Tribulation Period. So how can we, the church, subject ourselves to a satanic government and pray for it as we are now instructed to do? We cannot! Dr. J. Dwight Pentecost says in his book, *Things To Come, A Study of Biblical Eschatology,* "Because of the relationship of the church to governments in this age and because of the satanic control of governments in the 70th week (Tribulation Period), the church must be delivered before the satanic government manifests itself."[3] I believe Dr. Pentecost is on target with his assessment that the church must be raptured before the Tribulation Period begins.

Note: *Those who believe in a mid-Tribulation Rapture would say the first half (3.5 years) of the Tribulation is a time of peace, and the anti-Christ does not manifest his full evil and wickedness until the second half (3.5 years) of the Tribulation Period, so the church doesn't need to be raptured until the middle of the Tribulation. While I agree that the first half of the Tribulation Period will be a time of peace, I do not believe God would have us pray for a Satanic controlled government that will be in power during that time. He has told us to be on alert and resist the Devil because he seeks to devour us (1 Peter 5:8). Why would God tell us to do this and then ask us to pray for the Devil and his government during the Tribulation Period? I don't believe God would do that.*

3. The outline of the Book of Revelation reveals the church is NOT present on the Earth during the seven years of Tribulation. In the Book of Revelation, chapters 1-5 are Pre-Tribulation chapters, and the church is mentioned several times—1:11, 20; 2:7, 11, 17; 3:6, 13, 22. Revelation chapters 6-19 are Tribulation chapters, and the church is not mentioned one single time. In fact, look at Revelation 13:9: *"He who has an ear let him hear."* What is missing from the previous mentioned verses in Revelation chapters 2-3? What's missing is *"what the Spirit says to the churches."* Why is this phrase missing? Because the church is not there. It has been raptured. The Book of Revelation closes with chapters 20-22, and once again the people of Christ, the church, is mentioned.

4. The 144,000 Jewish witnesses are an indication that the church must be raptured before the Tribulation Period. Today, the church has been given the task through the Great Commission (Matthew 28:19-20) to take the gospel to the world. But Revelation 7 and 14 indicate that during the Tribulation Period 12,000 Jewish men from the 12 tribes of Israel are sent out to the nations of the world as witnesses for Christ, essentially to do what the church has been called to do today. Why would God raise up 144,000 witnesses to do the job of the church if the church was still on the earth during the Tribulation Period? He wouldn't. The only reason the 144,000 witnesses are commissioned to take the gospel to the world during the Tribulation Period is because the church has been raptured.

5. Old Testament believers Enoch and Elijah, who did not experience death, are examples of God rapturing believers from the Earth. In a similar way, God will rapture believers before the Tribulation Period, and like Enoch and Elijah, they will be raptured before they die (1 Thessalonians 4:17).

Hebrews 11:5: *By faith, Enoch was taken away so that he did not experience death, and he was not to be found because God took him away.*

2 Kings 2:11-12: *As they continued walking and talking, a chariot of fire with horses of fire suddenly appeared and separated the two of them. Then Elijah went up into heaven in the whirlwind.*

6. The restraining of the Holy Spirit on the anti-Christ is removed when the church is raptured.

*2 **Thessalonians** 2:7-8: For the mystery of lawlessness is already at work; but the one now restraining (Holy Spirit) will do so until he is out of the way, and then the lawless one (anti-Christ) will be revealed.*

Right now, the Holy Spirit is holding back the full work of Satan on the Earth. When the church is raptured, the Holy Spirit goes to Heaven with believers because the Holy Spirit dwells in believers. When the Holy Spirit is removed, the anti-Christ will be revealed to the world. Since he is revealed at the beginning of the Tribulation Period, it is my opinion, and that of many others, the church must be raptured before the Tribulation Period starts.

WHAT IS THE PURPOSE OF THE RAPTURE?

Rick Warren expressed in his book *The Purpose-Driven Life,* "You weren't put on earth to be remembered. You were put here to prepare for eternity."[4] That eternity begins at the Rapture. God has a purpose and a reason for everything He does. Solomon says as much in Ecclesiastes 3:1-15. If God has a purpose for everything, then He has a purpose for the Rapture. What is it?

The first purpose of the Rapture is to free believers from sin. 1 Corinthians 15:42-44 tells us that when the resurrection of dead believers takes place at the Rapture, we are finished with sin. Paul says we are, *"sown in corruption"* (sinful), *"raised in incorruption"* (sinless); *"sown in dishonor"* (sinful), *"raised in glory"* (sinless); *"sown in weakness"* (sinful), *"raised in power"* (sinless); *"sown a natural body"* (sinful), *"raised a spiritual body"* (sinless). No more sin. No more temptation. No more Satan.

The second purpose of the Rapture is to remove believers from the wrath of God. As we have already seen, believers are not meant to endure the Tribulation Period because we have been saved by the grace of God through Jesus Christ. The act of salvation guarantees us the protection from God's wrath on the Earth. Daniel says we will escape the Tribulation Period (12:1), and Paul says Jesus will rescue us from the Tribulation Period in 1 Thessalonians 1:10. Jesus tells us in His own words that He will keep us from His wrath in Revelation 3:10. All this points to the fact that all believing Christians will be removed before the Tribulation Period starts.

The third purpose of the Rapture is to usher believers into eternity. 1 Thessalonians 4:16-17 says believers will meet the Lord in the air and be with Him forever. Let that sink in for a moment. We will be with the Lord forever, and ever, and ever. Paul goes on to say in 2 Corinthians 5:8, *"We are confident, I say, and willing rather to be absent from the body, and to be present with the Lord"* (KJV).

It is important to understand that to be ushered into eternity with Jesus you must be a Christian. You must admit you're a sinner, believe that Jesus is God, confess your sins, and commit your life to Him. It's not just about saying you believe in God. Many people believe in God, but they have no relationship with Him. In any relationship there is commitment, communication, and interaction. What kind of marriage would Glynis and I have if there were no commitment, communication, or interaction with each other? Most would describe that as no relationship at all. Jesus desires a relationship with you and me. That's what makes Christianity different than any other religion. It's not a religion; it's a relationship. Do you have a relationship with Jesus?

WHAT'S GOD'S PLAN FOR THE RAPTURE?

The plan of the Rapture involves Jesus Himself. There will be a sudden descent that will bring Jesus to a point above the Earth in the sky.

> *1 Thessalonians 4:16: For the Lord Himself will descend from heaven with a shout, with the archangel's voice, and with the trumpet of God, and the dead in Christ will rise first.*

He is not sending an angel or a prophet, He is coming Himself. What a sight that is going to be when the first thing believers see the instant they are transformed from an earthly body to a heavenly body is Jesus (1 Corinthians 15:52). He will be in the sky; calling them up as He ushers them back to their heavenly home. There's a part of me that hopes I am alive when the Rapture happens, but if I'm not, it will be a glorious experience to be one of the first raised at the Rapture.

The plan of the Rapture involves three sounds: a shout, the archangel's voice, and the trumpet of God. I believe the shout is the voice of Jesus. Look what John 5:25 says: *"I assure you: An hour is coming, and is now here, when the dead will hear the voice of the Son of God, and those who hear will live."*

The archangel's voice is harder to determine. It could be Michael's voice that was mentioned in Daniel 12:1. While there is no concrete proof the archangel will be Michael, we do know there is an archangel present, and he will be speaking at the Rapture.

What is the trumpet of God? Paul is very clear that at the Rapture believers will be called up to Jesus at the sounding of a trumpet. We've already seen what 1 Thessalonians 4:16 says. Now look what 1 Corinthians 15:51-52 says: *"Listen! I am telling you a mystery: We will not all fall asleep, but we will all be changed, in a moment, in the twinkling of an eye, at the last trumpet. For the trumpet will sound, and the dead will be raised incorruptible, and we will be changed."*

The use of trumpet sounds was common in ancient Jewish culture. In fact, there are 62 references found in the Bible. The sounding of a trumpet was used to announce royalty, declare war, announce special times and seasons, and gather people for a journey.

During the Jewish festival of the Feast of Trumpets, the Jews would blow short trumpet blasts. They ended the feast with a long blast they called the last trump. Judaism has traditionally connected this last trump with the resurrection of the dead. Paul obviously makes this same connection. For many Jewish Christians, the association between the Rapture and the Feast of the Trumpets is so strong, they believe the Rapture will occur during the Feast of the Trumpets. What an appropriate instrument to announce our journey with Jesus to our home in Heaven.

The plan for the Rapture involves a great resurrection. The dead will be raised first (1 Thessalonians 4:16), then those who are alive, second. Note Paul's language in verse 17. He uses the personal pronoun *"we,"* which indicated he believed

Jesus would be returning in his lifetime. Furthermore, he does it again in 1 Corinthians 15:51. There was a common belief that Jesus' departure and return would be a very short period of time. There was a sense of urgency from Paul to the Thessalonians that Jesus could return at any moment. The same sense of urgency has not changed in 2,000 years. Christians still believe Jesus could return at any moment. One day the perfect moment will come. Will you be ready? Have you made your final reservation for your final destination?

Will Infants And Young Children, The Mentally Challenged, And Unborn Babies Be Involved In The Rapture?

The Apostle Paul tells us in Romans 3:23, *"For all have sinned and fall short of the glory of God."* "All" includes infants and children. We are ALL guilty before God because of the sin we inherited through our parents and grandparents from Adam and Eve. Look what David writes in Psalm 51:5, *"Indeed, I was guilty when I was born; I was sinful when my mother conceived me."* David knows that even in conception, he was sinful. Because infants and children die, it shows that even they have been impacted, both physically and spiritually, by Adam's sin. We all stand guilty before God, whether we are a child or an adult.

God is righteous and just, and the only way He can make a sinful person righteous is through the forgiveness of sin through Jesus Christ. The only way I can be forgiven of my sins is to accept Jesus Christ as my Savior. In John 14:6 Jesus says, *"I am the way, the truth, and the life; no one comes to the Father except through Me."* Salvation is an individual choice. While I am sinful because of inherited sin, I cannot be saved through my parent's salvation; I must make the choice for myself. The same goes for babies and young children.

But what if they never reach the ability to make an individual choice? The "Age of Accountability" teaches that those who die before reaching the ability to make an individual choice to accept or reject Christ are saved by God's grace and mercy. There is no specific age, the "Age of Accountability" covers. It varies from child to child.

The Bible passage we use to support this belief is 2 Samuel 12:21-23. In the context of this passage King David committed adultery with Bathsheba, which resulted in Bathsheba becoming pregnant. Nathan, the prophet, was sent by God to David to confront David because of his sin. Nathan informed David that God had determined the child would die as a result of David and Bathsheba's sin. David grieved and mourned, fasted and prayed that God would change His mind and spare the child. But once the child died, David ended his fasting and praying. His servants were puzzled by his actions, and in verse 21 asked him, *"What did you just do? While the baby was alive, you fasted and wept, but when he died, you got up and ate food."* David responded in verses 22-23, *"While the baby was alive, I fasted and wept because I thought, 'Who knows? The Lord may be gracious to me and let him live.' But now that he is dead, why should I fast? Can I bring him back again? I'll go to him, but he will never return to me."*

David's response shows us that those who cannot make that individual choice are safe with the Lord. David said he could not bring the child back, but that he will go to the child. David seemed comforted by the fact that one day he will see his child again in Heaven. God is a loving and gracious God, and it is my belief that while God applies sin to all men, even infants and children, He also applies forgiveness through Jesus for those babies, children, the mentally challenged, and the unborn in the wombs of their mothers, who are incapable of making an individual choice. If you've had a child that died, you should be comforted in believing they are safe in Heaven with Jesus. Why? Because we can always be sure God will do what is right, and in this case, the belief in the "Age of Accountability" is what is right.

How Does The Rapture Encourage Us Today?

Paul tells the Thessalonian believers in 1 Thessalonians 4:18, *"Therefore encourage one another with these words."* Paul's new revelation from the Lord was meant to encourage the Thessalonians and to answer their question about those who had died believing in the Lord. Consequently, how does the Rapture encourage us today?

First, the Rapture reminds us that death is not the end. To the world, death is grim and full of sorrow, but for the Christian, death is joyous and full of hope. As a pastor, I've officiated numerous funerals where I've seen this first hand. I remember getting a call from a funeral director that he needed someone to preach a graveside service for an elderly gentleman who had died. He was a World War II veteran and his wife had preceded him in death. I'd never met the man, his deceased wife, or his two daughters. When I arrived at the cemetery there were four people. The funeral director pulled me aside and told me I would be wise to make this as quick as possible. The four people, who were the two daughters and their boyfriends, almost got into a fistfight before I arrived. This man's death was bitter, angry, and hostile. I read Psalm 23, made a few comments, and said a prayer. It took all of seven minutes. Imagine that you live 70 years on this Earth and four people show up at your funeral. How sad!

In contrast, I have done many funerals for believers that were a celebration, a victory, a joyous passing from this life into eternity. One that comes to mind is Linda Brand, a member of the church I pastored from that same small town in Whitewright, Texas. Linda was a deacon's wife, the city librarian, and one of the kindest people I've ever met. She was a true believer. She passed away from a heart attack that occurred at our Thanksgiving dinner. Linda never regained consciousness and died a few days later. When we had her funeral at the church, we couldn't fit all the people in our sanctuary that seated over 300. It was standing room only. Linda had made a comment when she was alive that she would have to sell beer and peanuts to get people to come to her funeral. She would have been pleasantly surprised by the amount of people present. Her service was one of the most worshipful and uplifting services I've ever had the pleasure to experience. It was joyous and full of hope. That's what a believer's funeral should be. For the believer, death is a celebration because we know death is not the end; it is a new beginning.

Second, the Rapture reminds us that Jesus' resurrection guarantees our resurrection.

1 Corinthians 15:20-23: But now Christ has been raised from the dead, the firstfruits of those who have fallen asleep. For since death came through a man, the resurrection of the dead also comes through a man. For just as in Adam

all die, so also in Christ all will be made alive.
But each in his own order: Christ, the firstfruits;
afterward, at His coming, the people of Christ.

Verse 23 tells us Jesus is the first resurrection, and then His people will be resurrected when He returns.

Third, the Rapture reminds us we will be with the Lord always. Paul Azinger, PGA golfer, recalls a time he was in a Bible Study led by fellow PGA golfer, Larry Moody. Paul had recently been diagnosed with cancer. Larry reassured Paul there is life after death, and said to Paul, "Zinger, we're not in the land of the living going to the land of the dying. We're in the land of the dying trying to get to the land of the living."[5] I think his advice perfectly describes our life on Earth and our goal for eternity.

Fourth, the Rapture reminds us Jesus is coming again. When I was growing up in Louisville, Kentucky in the 70's, one of our favorite games to play was hide-n-seek. The person who was "It" would count to 30 and then say, "Ready or not, here I come." Then they would go searching for the other players who were hiding. One day Jesus will say, "Ready or not, here I come." Then He will return to the Earth calling for those who have committed their lives to Him. You may think you have time, but let me remind you there is an eternal deadline you have no control over, and that is the unannounced return of Jesus. The most important thing you can do is give your life to Jesus. Two thousand years ago, He promised He would rise on the third day, and He did. Throughout the Bible, He promises He is coming back, and He will.

This reminds me of a story about British explorer Sir Ernest Shackleton, who while on an expedition to the South

Pole, left a few men behind on Elephant Island, promising that he would return for them. Later, when he tried to go back, huge icebergs blocked the way to the island. But, as if a miracle from God, suddenly a channel opened up in the ice and the ship was able to get through. His men saw him coming and were ready and waiting. With no time to waste, quickly the men scrambled aboard, and as soon as the ship cleared the island than the ice closed behind them. Thinking about their fast departure, Shackleton said to his men, "It was fortunate you were all packed and ready to go!" To which they replied, "We never gave up hope. Whenever the sea was clear of ice, we rolled up our sleeping bags and reminded each other, 'The boss may come today.'"[6]

Jesus may come today. Are you ready?

7 POINTS OF REVIEW:

1. The Rapture is the resurrection of Christians both dead and alive, and it is a belief that is clearly taught in the Bible by both Jesus and the apostle Paul.

2. The Rapture is the next event on God's prophetic calendar, and it will take place before the start of the Tribulation Period.

3. The purpose of the Rapture is four-fold: First, to remove Christian believers before the Tribulation Period starts because we are not meant to experience the wrath of God. Second, to free believers from sin. Third, to begin God's judgment for evil, wickedness, and sin on the Earth. Fourth, to usher believers into Heaven.

4. When Jesus raptures Christian believers, He will do it Himself. He will not send an angel or a prophet; He is coming Himself.

5. The people involved in the Rapture are Jesus, the archangel, Christian believers (both dead and alive), babies, small children, the mentally challenged, and babies of pregnant mothers.

6. The Rapture proves that death is not the end of life. Believers will be resurrected to eternal life in Heaven.

7. The Rapture reminds Christians that Jesus' resurrection guarantees our resurrection, and when we are resurrected we will be with the Lord forever.

5 BIG QUESTIONS:

1. What are the three primary views of the Rapture mentioned in the chapter? Which view is supported in the chapter, and why?

_____

_____

_____

2. How many resurrections are mentioned in the chapter? When will each resurrection take place?

_____

_____

_____

3. What are the three parts of God's plan for the Rapture?

_____

_____

_____

4. Did the apostle Paul believe he would be alive when Jesus returned to Rapture the church? What two scriptures are cited as proof?

_____

_____

_____

5. How does the Rapture encourage you today?

_____

_____

_____

CHAPTER 2

THE NEW HEAVENLY BODY

For we know that if our earthly house, a tent, is
destroyed, we have a building from God, a house
not made with hands, eternal in the heavens.
2 Corinthians 5:1

We need to understand that death is not what God intended when He created man in His own image. He intended for us to be like Him, eternal, and the body He created for us was to last forever. The reason we are dying is not because of our body; it's because of our sin.

The Doctrine of Resurrection teaches that we are both physical and spiritual. Even though the soul is separated from the body at death, it's only temporary. Hank Hanegraaf in his book, *Resurrection,* says, "We see that the blueprint of our glorified bodies are in the bodies we now possess...Just as there is continuity between our earthly bodies and the bodies we had at birth...so too there will be continuity from death to resurrection...In fact without continuity, there is no point in even using the word resurrection."[7]

One of the great things about the Rapture is that one day all believers in Jesus will be changed, from an earthly body to a heavenly body; from a sinful body to a sinless body; from a natural body to a spiritual body. God is a triune being as Father, Son, and Holy Spirit, and He created us to be a triune being of body, soul, and spirit. The body does not change after we are saved. At salvation, our soul is rescued by God from Hell, and a new spirit is put within us. Ezekiel 36:26 says, *"And I will give you a new heart—I will give you new and right desires—and put a new spirit within you. I will take out your stony hearts of sin and give you new hearts of love"* (TLB).

WHAT IS THE NEW SPIRIT WITHIN YOU?

It's the Holy Spirit. He is sent by God, the Father. John 14:26 says, *"But the Counselor, the Holy Spirit—the Father will send Him in My name—will teach you all things and remind you of everything I have told you."*

1 Corinthians 15 is the Bible's most comprehensive teaching on the resurrection. In verse 35 the apostle Paul asks two questions, and then answers the two questions in verses 36-52. Let's take a look:

> But someone will say, "How are the dead raised? What kind of body will they have when they come?" Foolish one! What you sow does not come to life unless it dies. And as for what you sow—you are not sowing the future body, but only a seed, perhaps of wheat or another grain. But God gives it a body as He wants, and to each of the seeds its own body. Not all flesh is the same flesh; there is one flesh for humans, another for animals, another for birds, and another for fish. There are heavenly

26

bodies and earthly bodies, but the splendor of the heavenly bodies is different from that of the earthly ones. There is a splendor of the sun, another of the moon, and another of the stars; for star differs from star in splendor. So it is with the resurrection of the dead: Sown in corruption, raised in incorruption; sown in dishonor, raised in glory; sown in weakness, raised in power; sown a natural body, raised a spiritual body.

If there is a natural body, there is also a spiritual body. So it is written: The first man Adam became a living being; the last Adam became a life-giving Spirit. However, the spiritual is not first, but the natural; then the spiritual. The first man was from the earth and made of dust; the second man is from heaven. Like the man made of dust, so are those who are made of dust; like the heavenly man, so are those who are heavenly. And just as we have borne the image of the man made of dust, we will also bear the image of the heavenly man. Brothers, I tell you this: flesh and blood cannot inherit the kingdom of God, and corruption cannot inherit incorruption. Listen! I am telling you a mystery: We will not all fall asleep, but we will all be changed, in a moment, in the twinkling of an eye, at the last trumpet. For the trumpet will sound, and the dead will be raised incorruptible, and we will be changed.

How Are The Dead Raised?

Paul's first question from v. 35 shows that the transformed bodies of the dead in Christ have two characteristics.

First, the dead in Christ are raised to a real body. Paul uses four illustrations to describe the difference between your old earthly body and your new heavenly body. In the first illustration, Paul says that what you sow cannot come to life unless it dies. You cannot be resurrected to a new heavenly body unless you die. In the second illustration, Paul says that not all flesh is the same. There is one flesh for humans, then another flesh for animals, birds, and fish. Just as there are different kinds of flesh on Earth, there will also be different kinds of bodies in Heaven. Which leads us to the third illustration, the differences between earthly bodies and heavenly bodies. Earthly bodies are flesh; heavenly bodies are spirit. Earthly bodies are sinful; heavenly bodies are sinless. Earthly bodies are temporary; heavenly bodies are permanent. The final illustration is about the brightness among the sun, moon, and stars. While every believer is given a new heavenly body, some believers will differ from others because of the faithfulness and sacrifice they experienced while on Earth. It's important to note that the heavenly body we have will be the heavenly body God wants us to have (v. 38).

Second, the dead in Christ are raised to a recognizable body. We are still going to be ourselves with our same appearance and distinct personalities. At salvation, I was changed, but I was still Neale. At the Rapture, I will be changed again, but I will still be Neale, who I've always been and always will be.

This brings up the age-old question, "Will we know each other in Heaven?" My answer is absolutely YES! 1 Thessalonians 4:16-17 says at the Rapture there will be a great reunion of family, friends, and loved ones in the clouds as we meet the Lord in the air. Husbands will be reunited with their wives. Children will be reunited with their parents. Best friends will once again see each other. If I'm Neale now, and I'm Neale when I'm dead, and I will be Neale when I'm resurrected, then doesn't it make sense that those who know me now will also know me in eternity?

WHAT KIND OF BODY WILL THE RESURRECTED HAVE WHEN THEY COME?

Paul's second question in verse 35 shows the kind of body the dead in Christ will have when they return with Christ.

First, it will be a radically changed body. In verses 42-44 Paul uses the word *"sown"* to mean buried. There are four characteristics of the eternal heavenly body.

1. *"Immortal"* – The old body ages and dies, but the new body does not age and will never die.
2. *"Glorious"* – The old body is sinful, but the new body is sinless.
3. *"Power"* – The old body is weak because of sin, but the new body is strong because it does not sin.
4. *"Spiritual"* – The old body is of the Earth, but the new body is of Heaven.

Theologian R. A. Torrey said, "We will not be disembodied spirits in the world to come, but redeemed spirits, in redeemed bodies, in a redeemed universe."[8]

Second, the body the dead in Christ have when they return with Christ is the body they received at the Rapture. In 1 Corinthians 15:50-52, Paul states the old body is changed into the new body instantaneously at the Rapture. As you are vaporized from the earthly body, you are transformed into your spiritual heavenly body. It happens in the *"twinkling of an eye."* How fast is that?

Pastor David Dykes of Green Acres Baptist Church in Tyler, Texas, shared a story in a sermon entitled, "Are You Ready For The Rapture?" In this sermon, he recalls a time he was speaking to college students at a retreat in North Carolina. The students were engaged, taking notes and following along in their Bibles, except one guy. He was sitting by himself and he didn't even have a Bible or notebook. He looked like your typical nerd or geek. He had thick glasses and a plastic pocket protector in his shirt. He even had a calculator clipped to his belt. Pastor Dykes said, "When I made that statement about the *'twinkling of an eye'* being the time it takes light to travel from the front of your eyeball to the optic nerves, he whipped out his calculator and started pecking away on it. It was one of those old scientific calculators that had a little thermal printer built in, so I could hear the hum of the paper coming out of it. After the session, several students were talking to me and I noticed this nerdy kid in line. He came up and said, '.6 nanoseconds.' I said, 'Excuse me?' He shoved his glasses up on the bridge of his nose and continued. '.6 nanoseconds. That's how long a twinkling of an eye is.' He showed me his print out and said, 'Light travels at 186,234 miles per second, and I estimate the average eyeball is about 24 millimeters, so that's .6 nanoseconds.' I said, 'Wow. Is that fast?' He said, 'That's fast.'"[9]

The point is that at the Rapture you will be instantaneously changed. It will happen so fast that you will not be able to see it happen. In .6 nanoseconds you're transformed from a mortal, sinful, and weak earthly body, to an immortal, sinless, and powerful heavenly body. If you think you can live a worldly life and then at the last second, right before the Rapture get saved, you won't have enough time to react. That last second is not even a second; it's less than a nanosecond. You need to prepare to meet Jesus now before the Rapture happens, because you won't have time when it happens.

The truth is, our earthly bodies won't last forever. The moment we are born, we begin to die. The Grim Reaper visits everyone sooner or later. Just as God has given us a body fit for life on Earth, one day He is going to give us a body that is fit for life in Heaven. One day Jesus will return for His followers and when He does, He will transform us for eternity. But Paul says it this way in Philippians 3:20-21, *"... but our citizenship is in heaven, from which we also eagerly wait for a Savior, the Lord Jesus Christ. He will transform the body of our humble condition into the likeness of His glorious body, by the power that enables Him to subject everything to Himself."*

Founding Father Ben Franklin captured the spirit of Paul in his mock epitaph.

"The Body of
B. Franklin Printer;
like the cover of an old book,
Its contents torn out,
And stripped of its lettering and gilding,
lies here, food for worms.
Yet the work shall not be lost:

For it will (as he believed) appear once more,
In a new & more perfect edition,
corrected and amended
By the Author."¹⁰

WHAT DOES THE BIBLE TELL US ABOUT THIS IMMORTAL BODY THAT WE WILL HAVE FOR ETERNITY?

Actually, the Bible says a lot about the eternal body. Let me give you seven attributes about your brand-new heavenly body.

First, your heavenly body is controlled by the Holy Spirit. Right now, you have a body that is controlled by the flesh, or the sinful nature. James 1:13-15 says, *"Let no one say when he is tempted, I am tempted from God; for God is incapable of being tempted by [what is] evil and He Himself tempts no one. But every person is tempted when he is drawn away, enticed and baited by his own evil desire (lust, passions). Then the evil desire, when it has conceived, gives birth to sin, and sin, when it is fully matured, brings forth death"* (AMP).

There is a constant battle between the flesh and the spirit. It reminds me of a cartoon I saw as a child. The animated character had the devil pop up on one shoulder and an angel pop up on the other shoulder. The devil was telling the person to do wrong because it would be fun, but the angel was telling the person to do good because it was right. That's kind of how temptation works in our life. Imagine the Devil on one shoulder and an angel on the other shoulder, and both are telling you what to do. Or imagine yourself at a fork in the road, and you have a choice to take the path on the right and resist sin, or take the path on the left, and give in to sin.

In your new heavenly body, you won't have to struggle with that choice because the temptation to sin is nowhere to be found. In the new heavenly body, the Spirit will always win. The Spirit will dominate your thoughts all the time. Notice what 1 Corinthians 15:42-44 says: *"Sown in corruption"* (the old you), *"raised in incorruption"* (the new you); *"sown in dishonor"* (your sinful body), *"raised in glory"* (your sinless body); *"sown in weakness"* (your body now), *"raised in power"* (your future body); *"sown a natural body"* (your human body), *"raised a spiritual body"* (your heavenly body). At the resurrection, Jesus is going to take a mortal, dishonorable, weak, and sinful body and completely change it into an immortal, glorified, powerful, and sinless body where sin and temptation do not exist.

The second attribute about the heavenly body is that it will be like the resurrected body of Jesus.

> **1 Corinthians 15:49:** *And just as we have borne the image of the man made of dust, we will also bear the image of the heavenly man.*

> **Philippians 3:20-21:** *...but our citizenship is in heaven, from which we also eagerly wait for a Savior, the Lord Jesus Christ. He will transform the body of our humble condition into the likeness of His glorious body, by the power that enables Him to subject everything to Himself.*

> **1 John 3:2-3:** *Dear friends, we are God's children now, and what we will be has not yet been revealed. We know that when He appears, we will be like Him, because we will see Him as*

He is. And everyone who has this hope in Him purifies himself just as He is pure.

What do these three passages tell us about Jesus' resurrected body and our future resurrected body?

1. Jesus' resurrected body was a real physical body. Jesus appeared to the disciples in the Upper Room after his resurrection and said, *"Look at My hands and My feet, that it is I Myself! Touch Me and see, because a ghost does not have flesh and bones as you can see I have"* (Luke 24:39).

2. Jesus' resurrected body could be touched. Again, in Luke 24:39 He told the disciples to touch Him. Jesus' resurrected body had all the characteristics that a normal body does.

3. Jesus' resurrected body ate food. Luke 24:41-43 says, *"But while they still could not believe because of their joy and were amazed, He asked them, 'Do you have anything here to eat?' So they gave Him a piece of a broiled fish, and He took it and ate in their presence."*

4. Jesus resurrected body defied gravity. After walking with the two witnesses on the Road to Emmaus, Jesus arrived at their home and ate a meal together with them. When He blessed the meal, they recognized Him and He disappeared right before their eyes (Luke 24:31). Before this Jesus appeared to the disciples in a locked Upper Room. John 20:19 says, *"In the evening of that first day of the week, the disciples were gathered together with the doors locked because of their fear of the Jews. Then Jesus came, stood among them, and said to them, 'Peace to you!'"* A week later He suddenly appeared to them again. John 20:26-28

says, "*After eight days His disciples were indoors again, and Thomas was with them. Even though the doors were locked, Jesus came and stood among them. He said, 'Peace to you!' Then He said to Thomas, 'Put your finger here and observe My hands. Reach out your hand and put it into My side. Don't be an unbeliever, but a believer.' Thomas responded to Him, 'My Lord and my God!'*"

I believe that our new heavenly bodies will be like Jesus' resurrected body. Just as Jesus had the five senses in His resurrected body on Earth, so will we have them in our resurrected body in Heaven. We will have a body that can see, hear, smell, taste, and touch. When Jesus cooked fish on the shore for the disciples, it's safe to say He used all five senses. He used His eyes to see the fish and His hands to place the fish on the fire. He used His ears to hear the fish as it sizzled on the fire. He could smell the aroma of the fish as it cooked, and finally He tasted the fish as He ate with the disciples. I believe we will use our five senses in our new heavenly bodies, but at a more acute awareness. We will see the walls and the foundation of the New Jerusalem brighter and more vibrant than ever before. We will hear the busyness of the eternal city clear and crisp with eternal ears. We will touch and feel the sensation with spiritual fingers. We will taste the fruit of the heavenly city, and our taste buds will burst with flavor. In the heavenly city, we will take a deep breath and savor the aroma. Our senses will function at a new level we've never experienced in the earthly body. We will make new discoveries that we never thought existed. We will experience God and His eternity in ways that will far exceed our wildest imaginations.

The third attribute about the new heavenly body is that it will be an eternal body. The Bible states over and over again and again that believers have been promised eternal life (Matthew 19:29; 25:46; John 3:16, 36; 6:40; 11:25-26; Galatians 6:8; 1 John 5:11, 13). Many wonder what age we will be in the new heavenly body? One theory is that since Jesus died at about 33 years of age, and since we will have a body like His resurrected body, then we will all be about 33 years old in eternity. Here's what I believe: We will be an age where age doesn't matter. I believe when you and I are ushered into Heaven after the Great White Throne Judgment, it will be in a body that does not age.

The fourth attribute about the new heavenly body is that it will be flesh and bone. Luke 24:39 has already shown us that Jesus' resurrected body is not a ghost but has flesh and bone. The same goes for you and me. In our resurrected body we will have substance. We will have a skeletal system. We will have bone for height and depth. We will have flesh to give us our appearance. Look what Job says in Job 19:25-27: *"But I know my living Redeemer, and He will stand on the dust at last. Even after my skin has been destroyed, yet I will see God in my flesh. I will see Him myself; my eyes will look at Him, and not as a stranger. My heart longs within me."*

Job tells us that in his eternal body, he will see God in his flesh. This flesh will not be like the flesh we have today; it will be a new, glorious flesh we will have for all eternity.

We won't experience diabetes, cancer, asthma, arthritis, osteoporosis, heart disease, hemophilia, MS, or ALS. Diseases will be non-existent in Heaven. Will we be beautiful and good looking? Absolutely, but not based on earthly standards or individual cultures, but based on what God considers beautiful. Our heavenly appearance will be pleasing to God, others, and ourselves. We won't look in the mirror and feel insecure. We won't wish we had a different nose or higher cheekbones or smaller ears. We won't try to impress others with our appearance. We won't need to, because we will all be beautiful, just as the Creator intended us to be. And we will never lose the health and beauty He has given us.

The fifth attribute about the new heavenly body is that it will be a glorified body. What does "glorified" mean? In the Bible it means beautiful, but it can also mean "to shine" or "to give off light." There are two occasions in the Bible where Jesus' body was transformed to give off light. First at the Transfiguration in Matthew 17:1-13, when Jesus took Peter, James, and John up the mountain and He was transformed so that Moses and Elijah appeared with Him before the three disciples. I believe a purpose for the Transfiguration was to give the disciples a glimpse of Jesus' resurrected body. The second occasion was on the Damascus Road in Acts 9, when Saul (Paul) was on his way to Damascus to persecute Christians. On his way he had an encounter with Jesus. Paul saw a great light and heard the voice of Jesus. The light was so great that it blinded him. Could we have a body in eternity that shines and gives off light? It's possible. Consider the following verses from the Bible:

> ***Daniel 12:3:*** *And those who are wise-the people of God-shall shine as brightly as the sun's brilliance, and those who turn many to righteousness will glitter like stars forever. (TLB)*

Matthew 5:14: *You are the world's light-a city on a hill, glowing in the night for all to see. (TLB)*

Philippians 2:14-15: *Do everything without grumbling and arguing, so that you may be blameless and pure, children of God who are faultless in a crooked and perverted generation, among whom you shine like stars in the world.*

The sixth attribute about the new heavenly body is it will be recognizable. As I have already stated from 1 Corinthians 15, I believe we will have our own distinct characteristics. I believe we will be us, the same person we were on Earth, albeit in a new eternal body. I will be recognized as me, and you will be recognized as you, and we will recognize those who we know from Earth. When Moses and Elijah appeared with Jesus at the Transfiguration, they were themselves, and the disciples recognized them as Moses and Elijah, distinct individuals, the same people they were when they walked on the Earth, but in a new heavenly body. What made me Neale on Earth is what will make me Neale in Heaven. You and I will have our personalities, our passions, our gifts, talents, and abilities. The things that interested us on Earth will interest us in Heaven. The traits that make us who we are on Earth are the same traits that will make us who we are in Heaven. Remember, once Jesus removed the veil of who He was after His resurrection, many people recognized Him (1 Corinthians 15:3-7).

People often think when they die that they will become an angel in Heaven. Nothing could be farther from the truth. Randy Alcorn says in his book *Heaven*, "Death is a relocation of the same person from one place to another. The place changes, but the person remains the same. The same person who becomes absent from his or her body becomes present with the Lord (2 Corinthians 5:8). The person who departs is the one who goes to be with Christ (Philippians 1:23)."[11] The Bible clearly teaches in 1 Corinthians 6:2-3 that humans will govern angels in Heaven. How can we lead and rule over angels if we are angels? The answer is we can't. So it's important to understand that angels are angels and redeemed humans are humans in Heaven.

The seventh and final attribute about the new heavenly body is that it will be unlimited by time, space, and gravity. If our new resurrected bodies are like Jesus' resurrected body, then we will have the ability to appear and disappear at will. We will think it and instantly be there. We will travel by will of the Spirit. On Earth, the Spirit dwells in the physical body, and the body transports the Spirit from one place to another. In our resurrected body, the Spirit is in control, and the Spirit transports the body. The resurrected body is not limited by the same things as our earthly body. In Luke 24:31-36 and John 20:19-26, Jesus appeared and disappeared as He willed. I believe it's possible that you and I may have that same ability.

What we do know for sure is that this present body will be radically changed. You will be transformed from a sinful body to a sinless body, from a body fit for Earth to a body fit for Heaven, from a body controlled by the flesh to a body controlled by the Spirit. This new resurrected body will be immortal, glorified, and powerful. It will be like Jesus' resurrected body. What is broken will be fixed. What is paralyzed will be un-paralyzed. What is diseased will be healed. What is crooked will become straight.

Joni Eareckson Tada, paralyzed in a diving accident as a teenager, says this about her heavenly body in her book *Heaven, Your Real Home*: "Somewhere in my broken, paralyzed body is the seed of what I shall become. The paralysis makes what I am to become all the more grand when you contrast atrophied, useless legs against splendorous resurrected legs. I'm convinced that if there are mirrors in heaven (and why not?), the image I'll see will be unmistakably "Joni," although a much better, brighter Joni. So much so, that it's not worth comparing...I will bear the likeness of Jesus, the man from heaven."[12]

Awaiting you in eternity is a new you, a better you. A you that is not limited by the flesh or sin, but unlimited and controlled by the Spirit. A body that is fit for life in Heaven, and what a glorious life that will be!

7 POINTS OF REVIEW

1. At the Rapture, you and I will be changed from an earthly sinful body to a heavenly sinless body.

2. 1 Corinthians 15 is the most comprehensive teaching on the resurrection in the Bible. In the chapter, Paul proves Jesus' resurrection, guarantees our resurrection, and explains how we will be resurrected.

3. Right now, in your earthly body, your sinful nature controls much of your thoughts and actions. In the new heavenly body, your thoughts and actions will be controlled by the Spirit all the time.

4. The new heavenly body is a real body. It will have a skeletal system. It will have flesh and bone to give it substance and structure. It is every bit a body, but a new eternal body. Just as you have a body that is fit for life on Earth, you will have a body that is fit for life in Heaven.

5. In the new heavenly body, you will be you. You will be recognized in Heaven. The same gifts, talents, and abilities you have on Earth you will have in Heaven. The same things that interest you on Earth will interest you in Heaven. You will be you and you will not be an angel.

6. On Earth, the Spirit is in the flesh, and the flesh transports the Spirit from one place to another. In your heavenly body, the Spirit is in control, and the Spirit transports the body.

7. In your heavenly body, what is broken will be fixed. What is paralyzed will be un-paralyzed. What is diseased will be healed. What is crooked will become straight.

5 BIG QUESTIONS

1. Using a dictionary, look up the definitions of "reincarnation" and "resurrection." How is resurrection better?

_____

_____

_____

2. What are the 4 characteristics of the heavenly body?

_____

_____

_____

3. The change from the earthly body to the heavenly body is instantaneous. How does Paul describe it in 1 Corinthians 15:52? How fast does Pastor Dykes' nerdy friend say it will be?

_____

_____

_____

4. What does Jesus' resurrected body reveal to us about our resurrected body?

_____

_____

_____

5. Your new heavenly body will be a glorified body. What does that mean?

_____

_____

_____

CHAPTER 3

THE JUDGMENT SEAT OF CHRIST

The Judgment seat "is meant for us professing Christians, real and imperfect Christians; and it tells us that there are degrees in that future blessedness proportioned to present faithfulness."[3]
Alexander Maclaren, 1826-1910.

"Jesus is your friend, not your judge." This was the tag line of a church's advertising campaign in a north Texas community. While I absolutely agree that Jesus is our friend, you need to know He is also our judge. Make no mistake, one day we will all stand before Jesus and He will judge us on our works, our stewardship, how we treated others, the things we did and didn't do, and much, much more. Hebrews 9:27 says, *"Just as it is destined that men die only once, and after that comes judgment" (TLB)*. Every human being born into the world, past, present, and future will one day stand in judgment before Jesus. Everyone will recognize Jesus as the "King of Kings and Lord of Lords." Paul tells us in Philippians 2:10, *"...that at the name of Jesus every knee will bow-of those who are in heaven and on earth, and under the earth."*

The Bible mentions three judgments. First, there is the Judgment Seat of Christ, which we will study in this chapter. It occurs after the Rapture in Heaven and is for believers only. Second, there is the Nations or Gentile Judgment, which will occur at the Second Coming of Jesus and is for those who take the mark of the beast (666) during the Tribulation Period. We will study this judgment in chapters five and six. The last judgment is The Great White Throne Judgment. It occurs at the end of the millennial reign of Christ, and is for unbelievers. We will study this judgment in chapter nine.

It's important to understand that none of these three judgments determine whether you are lost or saved. In fact, no judgment does that. You make that determination before you reach the judgment. If you accept Jesus before the Rapture, then your judgment will be in Heaven at the Judgment Seat of Christ. If you think doing nothing is the right decision, you would be wrong, because no decision about Jesus is really a decision to reject Him.

In this chapter, let's focus on the Judgment Seat of Christ for believers. It is also called the Bema Judgment. Bema comes from the Greek word that illustrates an athlete standing to receive his reward for being victorious in ancient Olympic games. As believers, you and I will stand before Jesus victorious over sin, and our reward will be eternity in Heaven with Jesus.

There are three main Scripture passages in which the apostle Paul talks about the Judgment Seat of Christ.

> *Romans 14:9-12: Christ died and came to life for this: that He might rule over both the dead and the living. But you, why do you criticize your brother? Or you, why do you look down*

on your brother? For we will all stand before the judgment seat of God. For it is written: As I live, says the Lord, every knee will bow to Me, and every tongue will give praise to God. So then, each of us will give an account of himself to God.

2 Corinthians 5:10: *For we must all appear before the judgment seat of Christ, so that each may be repaid for what he has done in the body, whether good or bad.*

1 Corinthians 3:10-15: *According to God's grace that was given to me, as a skilled master builder I have laid a foundation, and another builds on it. But each one must be careful how he builds on it, because no one can lay any other foundation than what has been laid—that is, Jesus Christ. If anyone builds on the foundation with gold, silver, costly stones, wood, hay, or straw, each one's work will become obvious, for the day will disclose it, because it will be revealed by fire; the fire will test the quality of each one's work. If anyone's work that he has built survives, he will receive a reward. If anyone's work is burned up, it will be lost, but he will be saved; yet it will be like an escape through fire.*

The "day" mentioned in verse 13 and the "reward" mentioned in verse 14, both refer to the Judgment Seat of Christ. In all three of these passages, it is important to note that Paul is writing to Christians, which tells us this judgment is for believers only. And because it is for believers only, this judgment is NOT about sin. Why? Because our sins have been forgiven and we are no longer under condemnation for sin.

> **Romans 8:1:** *Therefore, no condemnation now exists for those in Christ Jesus.*

Revelation 21-22 speaks extensively about Heaven and nowhere does it mention sin, in fact just the opposite. We know that sin cannot inhabit Heaven.

> **Revelation 21:27:** *Nothing profane will ever enter it: no one who does what is vile or false, but only those written in the Lamb's book of life.*

> **Revelation 22:14-15:** *Blessed are those who wash their robes, so that they may have the right to the tree of life and may enter the city by the gates. Outside are the dogs, the sorcerers, the sexually immoral, the murderers, the idolaters, and everyone who loves and practices lying.*

When it comes to judgment and judging others, let me make three important points. First, we misinterpret the meaning of Matthew 7:1 – *"Do not judge, so that you won't be judged."* I call this humanity's favorite verse, because we quote this verse anytime someone starts to judge us concerning our attitudes or our actions. We think it means that we are never to make a judgment about people. That's not true. God has given us a brain and He expects us to use that brain, sometimes to judge those in our life. The truth is, we make judgments about people every day. We judge whether we want them in our life or not. We judge whether we want them around our children or not. We judge whether they will draw us to God, or drive us away from God. What Matthew 7:1 really means is that you and I will not be the ones to judge whether someone is ultimately lost or saved. That's between them and God. But we are to judge others, not condemningly, but simply to decide whether we want them in our life and the life of our family. There is nothing wrong with that.

Second, in life you will run into the self-appointed judges. It is impossible to appease them. They are toxic people. You need to remove them from your life as quickly as possible. If Matthew 7:1 is humanity's favorite verse, then Matthew 7:5 is humanity's least favorite verse: Jesus calls the self-appointed judges, *"Hypocrite!"* and tells them, *"First take the log out of your eye, and then you will see clearly to take the speck out of your brother's eye."* Sadly, I have run into a hand full of these toxic, self-appointed judges in my 30-plus years of ministry. Some of them have even been in the churches I have served. I learned that I could never please them, and the best thing I can do is remove them from my life. On one occasion that meant removing myself from the place of their influence. But it only took God two weeks to open a door for me to continue my calling as a pastor. Two weeks after I resigned, I received a call to fill in at a church whose pastor just retired. This church hired me as their interim pastor, and four months later the church called me as their full-time pastor. It is a joy to serve God and the people of this church. Has there been a job in your life that made you miserable, that you hated getting up every day and going to work? If so, then you understand. Remember, pastors are people, too. We struggle just like you. And sometimes those struggles are with people, even Christian people.

The final clarification I want to make about judgment and judging others is that the only one you and I have to answer to for this life is Jesus, the true Judge. You don't have to answer to the self-appointed toxic judges in the world. One day, if you are a believer, you will stand before the Judgment Seat of Christ, and Jesus will lay out your life before you and will judge you, not on your sins, as they have been forgiven, but on your stewardship.

Paul shows in 1 Corinthians 3:14-15 that some works will be burned up because the motive was not godly, but some works will be rewarded because the motive was godly. Ask yourself, "Why do I teach my Bible Study class? Because I want everyone to know I'm a great teacher?" Wrong motive! That work will be burned up when you stand before Jesus. Or, do you teach that Bible Study class in order to make disciples and teach the truth of God's word? Right motive! That work will be rewarded when you stand before Jesus.

Am I working for the Lord? Am I giving my best? Am I giving glory to Jesus? Deep down in your heart, your soul, and your mind, you know your motive behind what you do. But if you don't, Jesus does, and one day you will stand before the Judgment Seat of Christ and give an account of the things done in your body.

WHO WILL BE INVOLVED IN THE JUDGMENT SEAT OF CHRIST?

There will only be two people involved in this judgment. First and foremost, there is Jesus, the Judge. The Father made Him judge, and He has a right to judge because He is without sin.

John 5:22, 27: *The Father, in fact, judges no one but has given all judgment to the Son ... And He has granted Him the right to pass judgment, because He is the Son of Man.*

Jesus will judge us, having walked in our shoes.

Hebrews 4:15: *For we do not have a high priest who is unable to sympathize with our weaknesses, but One who has been tested in every way as we are, yet without sin.*

The second group of people involved in The Judgment Seat of Christ will be raptured believers. There will be no unbelievers at this judgment. Notice in Romans 14:10-12, Paul's use of the personal pronouns *"you," "your," "we,"* and *"us."*

Romans 14:10-12: *But you, why do you criticize your brother? Or you, why do you look down on your brother? For we will all stand before the judgment seat of God. For it is written: As I live, says the Lord, every knee will bow to Me, and every tongue will give praise to God. So then, each of us will give an account of himself to God.*

Paul is obviously speaking to believers in these verses.

WHAT IS THE PURPOSE OF THE
JUDGMENT SEAT OF CHRIST?

It is to give an account of ourselves to God.

Romans 14:12: *So then, each of us will give an account of himself to God.*

When we stand before Jesus, there will be no arguing. There will be no negotiating. There will be no justifying our actions. Jesus will know exactly what we did and why we did it. He will understand the motives behind the choices we made. It's not just the action of our choices that will concern Jesus. He will also be concerned with the motives behind those choices.

This reminds me of the story of Ananias and Sapphira in Acts 5:1-11. The Christian church was just getting started, and many of the new believers were selling land and property and giving it to the apostles to distribute to those in need. Joseph, also called Barnabas, sold a piece of property he owned, brought the money and laid it at the apostle's feet (Acts 4:36-37). Ananias and Sapphira probably saw the reaction Joseph got from the apostles and they did the same, but they didn't give all the money to the apostles; instead they kept back a portion for themselves. We don't know exactly why they didn't give all the money. Maybe they received more than they expected for the property. Whatever the reason, it caused them to lie to the Holy Spirit. When Ananias brought the proceeds to the apostles, Peter knew what Ananias had done and questioned him about it. Ananias had to give an account for his choice and the motive behind that choice. When he lied to the Holy Spirit, it cost him his life. Three hours later, Sapphira, unaware of Ananias' death, came before Peter. When confronted by her choice to lie to the Holy Spirit, she died just like her husband.

Our choices, and the motives behind those choices, will probably not result in our death. However, like Ananias and Sapphira, we will have to give an account for those choices one day. That day for the Christian believer will be at The Judgment Seat of Christ.

WHAT IS JESUS CONCERNED WITH AT THE JUDGMENT SEAT OF CHRIST?

First, let's look at what He's not concerned with. He will not be concerned with punishing you because of your sin. When you accepted Jesus as Savior, He forgave you for all your sins—past, present, and future.

> **Psalm 103:12:** As far as the east is from the west, so far has He removed our transgressions from us.

> **Hebrews 8:12:** For I will be merciful to their wrongdoing, and I will never again remember their sins.

> **Hebrews 10:17:** I will never again remember their sins and their lawless acts.

> **1 John 1:7:** But if we walk in the light as He Himself is in the light, we have fellowship with one another, and the blood of Jesus His Son cleanses us from all sin.

All these verses clearly show that Jesus is not concerned with punishing you because of your sins. The whole reason He went to the cross was to forgive you, to remove the penalty of death from you, and to give you eternal life.

Let's look at the most famous verse in the Bible and the two companion verses that follow it.

> **John 3:16-18:** *For God so loved the world, that he gave his only begotten Son, that whosoever believeth in him should not perish, but have everlasting life. For God sent not his Son into the world to condemn the world; but that the world through him might be saved. He that believeth on him is not condemned: but he that believeth not is condemned already, because he hath not believed in the name of the only begotten Son of God. (KJV)*

Let me make four simple but essential points about this passage:

1. Jesus loves you so much that He was willing to die in your place.
2. Those who believe in Jesus will receive eternal life and will spend this eternity with Him.
3. Jesus did not come to condemn the world, but to save the world.
4. Those who believe in Jesus right now are not condemned, but those who don't believe are already condemned. That condemnation changes only if they believe.

Now that you understand what Jesus will not be concerned with, let's look at what He will be concerned with.

He will be concerned with the reasons why you did the things you did. A lot of what we think are good works will be burned up because our reason for doing them was selfish and ungodly (1 Corinthians 3:11-15).

Who determines the reasons behind the things you do? Jesus does, because He knows the heart and soul of every person. You may not be sure if the reason you went on the mission trip was a pure motive, but Jesus does. He knows every reason and every motive for every choice and every decision you ever made in your entire life. There will be no questioning Jesus because He is the supreme Judge, and He knows it all.

Jesus will also be concerned with the things that you should have done, but did not do. James 4:17 says, *"So any person who knows what is right to do but does not do it, to him it is sin" (AMP)*. A faithful steward gets the job done. An unfaithful steward doesn't.

Early in our marriage Glynis told me that I suffer from the "Big P." What she meant, was that I suffer from procrastination. She was right! There were things that I should have done that I didn't do, mostly because I didn't want to do them. I kept putting them off. I discovered that putting things off didn't make them go away, it just made them harder to do when I finally got around to it. The same goes in our Christian life. When God gives you a task to do, don't put it off—go do it. He's given it to you at that moment, and you need to trust that His timing is always perfect.

How Will Believers Be Judged At the Judgment Seat of Christ?

First, you will be judged graciously. The Judgment Seat of Christ is not about convicting you for your sins; it's about reminding you that you are a steward of the Christian life. Jesus is not about beating you down; He will be about lifting you up. He won't be angry at the judgment, but maybe more disappointed.

When I was a child, I always wanted to do the right thing because I didn't want to disappoint my parents. I didn't want to see that look on their faces when I stood before them with my head hung in shame because I made a bad choice. I still feel that way today with regards to my wife and children. I know they will love me regardless, but I don't want to put them in that position. The same goes for God. He will love me no matter what. He's my Heavenly Father.

Second, you will be judged thoroughly. When you stand before Jesus, He won't judge you just on the terrible things you did; He will judge you also on the good things you did. He will remind you of all the people you witnessed to and helped lead to the Lord. He will remind you of all those you ministered to and helped in their time of need. He will remind you of all the times you made the Sabbath a day of rest and worship, and all the times you read, prayed, and applied His Word to your life. He will remind you of all the times you obeyed Him and followed His will in your life. He will remind you of all the times you acted with grace and mercy to those in your life. He will remind you of all the times you said the right thing and acted in the right way. When you stand before Jesus at this judgment, it will be a complete judgment. There will be no stone left unturned, and everything will be brought to light.

Third, you will be judged impartially. Romans 2:11 says, *"There is no favoritism with God."* No special advantages will be given to the rich. Those who received perks and power in this life will find themselves stripped of every crutch. Ministers and missionaries will not be given preferential treatment. In fact, those who teach the Word of God will be held to a stricter judgment (James 3:1). The color of your skin, the size of your bank account, your fame and fortune will hold no value with the One who *"...is a discerner of the thoughts and intents of the heart"* (Hebrews 4:12, KJV).

Finally, you will be judged individually. 2 Corinthians 5:10 says, *"For we must all appear before the judgment seat of Christ, so that each may be repaid for what he has done in the body, whether good or bad."* I will take responsibility for the stewardship of my life, and you will take responsibility for the stewardship of your life. I won't be judged for your stewardship, and you won't be judged for my stewardship.

WHAT ARE BELIEVERS JUDGED FOR?

Let's look again at 1 Corinthians 3:12-13: *"If anyone builds on the foundation with gold, silver, costly stones, wood, hay, or straw, each one's work will become obvious, for the day will disclose it, because it will be revealed by fire; the fire will test the quality of each one's work."*

As believers, you and I will be judged for the works that are revealed by fire: gold, silver, and precious stones.

- How we treated others: **Matthew 10:41-42:** *Anyone who welcomes a prophet because he is a prophet will receive a prophet's reward. And anyone who welcomes* *a righteous person because he's righteous will receive a righteous person's reward. And whoever gives just a cup of cold water to one of these little ones because he is a disciple —I assure you: He will never lose his reward!*

- How we used our spiritual gift: **1 Peter 4:10:** *Based on the gift they have received, everyone should use it to serve others, as good managers of the varied grace of God.*

- How we spent our money: **1 Timothy 6:17-19:** *Charge them that are rich in this world, that they be not highminded, nor trust in uncertain riches, but in the living God, who giveth us richly all things to enjoy; That they do good, that they be rich in good works, ready to distribute, willing to communicate; up in store for themselves a good foundation against the time to come, that they may lay hold on eternal life. (KJV)*

- How we spent our time: **Ephesians 5:15-16:** *Pay careful attention, then, to how you walk—not as unwise people but as wise—making the most of the time, because the days are evil.*

- How much we suffered for Jesus: **Matthew 5:11-12:** *Blessed are you when they insult you and persecute you and falsely say every kind of evil against you because of Me. Be glad and rejoice, because your reward is great in heaven. For that is how they persecuted the prophets who were before you.* **Romans 8:18:** *For I consider that the sufferings of this present time are not worth comparing with the glory that is going to be revealed to us.* **2 Corinthians 4:17:** *For our momentary light affliction is producing for us an absolutely incomparable eternal weight of glory.*

Fired from your job because of your faith in Jesus? Overlooked for that promotion because of your religious convictions? Bypassed from the company perks because you're a Christian? God sees it all and will make everything right.

WHAT ARE THE RESULTS OF THE JUDGMENT SEAT OF CHRIST?

Some Christians will suffer loss. Why? Because the motive behind the action was ungodly.

> **2 John 8:** *Watch yourselves so that you don't lose what we have worked for, but you may receive a full reward.*

There are two interpretations of this verse:

1. A Christian backslider will lose his reward. Saved and in Heaven, but not rewarded.
2. If you do not accomplish the things God has for you to do, you will not receive a full reward.

> **1 Corinthians 3:15:** *If anyone's work is burned up, it will be lost, but he will be saved; yet it will be like an escape through fire.*

While some Christians will suffer loss, other Christians will receive rewards. I believe that our rewards will be literal crowns. The Bible mentions five crowns:

- An Incorruptible Crown. This crown is for those that overcame selfish desires of the flesh.

  1 Corinthians 9:25-27: And every man that striveth for the mastery is temperate in all things. Now they do it to obtain a corruptible crown; but we an incorruptible. I therefore so run, not as uncertainly; so fight I, not as one that beateth the air: But I keep under my body, and bring it into subjection: lest that by any means, when I have preached to others, I myself should be a castaway. (KJV)

  Paul was not afraid he would lose his salvation, but he was afraid that he could lose his reward, or be "...disqualified for the prize."

- A Crown of Rejoicing. This crown is for those who have witnessed and won people to the Lord. Also known as the "Soul Winner's Crown."

  1 Thessalonians 2:19-20: For what is our hope, or joy, or crown of rejoicing? Are not even ye in the presence of our Lord Jesus Christ at his coming? For ye are our glory and joy. (KJV)

- The Crown of Life. This crown is for those Christians who overcame intense suffering or trials of life. Sometimes called the "Martyr's Crown."

  Revelation 2:10: Fear none of those things which thou shalt suffer: behold, the devil shall cast some of you into prison, that ye may be tried; and ye shall have tribulation ten days: be thou faithful unto death, and I will give thee a crown of life. (KJV)

- The Crown of Righteousness. This crown is for those Christians who look for the day when Jesus will call for His saints at the Rapture. The Apostle Paul believed this would be his crown.

  *2 **Timothy 4:8:** Henceforth there is laid up for me a crown of righteousness, which the Lord, the righteous judge, shall give me at that day: and not to me only, but unto all them also that love his appearing. (KJV)*

- The Crown of Glory. This crown is for the faithful preachers and teachers who have been diligent to feed the sheep of God. This crown is also known as the "Pastor's Crown."

  *1 **Peter 5:2-4:** Feed the flock of God which is among you, taking the oversight thereof, not by constraint, but willingly; not for filthy lucre, but of a ready mind; neither as being lords over God's heritage, but being ensamples to the flock. And when the chief Shepherd shall appear, ye shall receive a crown of glory that fadeth not away. (KJV)*

All these crowns will be used to glorify God. I believe they are literal crowns we will wear on the head of the new glorified body.

Revelation 4:9-11: Whenever the living creatures give glory, honor, and thanks to the One seated on the throne, the One who lives forever and ever, the 24 elders fall down before the One seated on the throne, worship the One who lives forever and ever, cast their crowns before the throne, and say: Our Lord and God, You are worthy to receive glory and honor and power, because You have created all things, and because of Your will they exist and were created.

Let me close this chapter on The Judgment Seat of Christ with the words of James Denney, Scottish theologian and preacher from the early 1900s. He said, "It is Christians only who are in view here. All that we have hidden shall be revealed. The things we have done in the body will come back to us, whether good or bad. Every pious thought, and every thought of sin; every secret prayer, and every secret curse; every unknown deed of charity, and every hidden deed of selfishness; we will see them all again, and though we have not remembered them for years, and perhaps have forgotten them altogether, we shall have to acknowledge that they are our own. Is not that a solemn thing to stand at the end of life?"[14] I believe it is!

7 POINTS OF REVIEW:

1. The Judgment Seat of Christ is only for the saved of the church. The unsaved will be judged at the Nations Judgment (also called the Gentile Judgment at the Second Coming of Christ—chapter 6) or at the Great White Throne Judgment after the millennial reign (chapter 9).

2. Since the Judgment Seat of Christ is for Christians only, then only Christ and Christians will be involved in this judgment.

3. At the Judgment Seat of Christ, there will be no negotiating. There will be no justifying our actions. Jesus will know exactly what we did and why we did it. He will not just be concerned with the actions behind our choices, but He will also be concerned with the motives behind those choices.

4. At the Judgment Seat of Christ, Jesus will not be concerned with punishing you, because all your sins have been forgiven past, present, and future. He will be concerned with the things you should have done but did not do.

5. At the Judgment Seat of Christ, believers will be judged thoroughly, impartially, individually, and graciously.

6. 1 Corinthians 3:10-15 teaches that at the Judgment Seat of Christ, your works will be revealed by fire.

If your works are good they will be rewarded (gold, silver, and precious stones). If your works are bad they will be burned up (wood, hay, and straw). Jesus is the only one who will determine whether your works are good or bad.

7. The results of the Judgment Seat of Christ are that some Christians may lose their reward, or not receive a full reward (2 John 8). Other Christians will receive a reward that may be a literal crown they will wear on the head of their new heavenly body for the sole purpose of glorifying God.

5 BIG QUESTIONS:

1. Why is Matthew 7:1 humanity's favorite verse and Matthew 7:5 humanity's least favorite verse?

_____

_____

_____

2. What mistake did Ananias and Sapphira make that Joseph (Barnabas) did not make?

_____

_____

_____

   Why was Ananias and Sapphira's choice, and the motive behind their choice, important when the Holy Spirit judged them in Acts 5?

_____

_____

What does this account tell you about your choices and the motives behind your choices?

_____

_____

3. Why will teachers of God's Word be held to a stricter judgment when they face Jesus at the Judgment Seat of Christ?

_____

_____

_____

4. What are some of the works you will be judged for at the Judgment Seat of Christ?

_____

_____

_____

5. What crowns are mentioned as rewards for believers?

_____

_____

_____

CHAPTER 4

A MARRIAGE MADE FOR HEAVEN

"You must be divorced from your sin, or
you cannot be married to Christ."[15]
Charles H. Spurgeon, 1834-1892

As a pastor, I have performed a lot of weddings. Some have been simple gatherings in the backyard or at a community gazebo. Others have been very formal affairs at the church or at a wedding venue. I have married couples where it was just them, two witnesses, and myself. I have married couples where the church was packed. Some of these weddings have been inexpensive, and some have cost thousands of dollars. I've married friends, I've married strangers, and I've married people who have served on staff with me. I've married my son, Roger, and his wife, Ashton. I've even had the pleasure of renewing the vows of my parents at their 50th anniversary. I've discovered that every wedding has one thing in common—excitement! It doesn't matter who, what, when, where, or why. At every wedding there is a sense of excitement. This newly married couple is excited to begin a life together. They are looking forward to moving into their home and someday adding children to the family. They are excited about just being together. They want to spend every waking moment with each other. In short, they just can't seem to get enough of each other.

In 1985 Glynis and I exchanged vows with one another in the chapel at First Baptist Church of Bonham, Texas. In attendance were our families, our friends, and our classmates from high school and college. We were both nervous and yet excited, because we had been preparing a long time for this day. I was marrying my best friend, and she was marrying the man of her dreams (those are her words, not mine)! We exchanged vows in front of a room full of witnesses and began a life together.

One day, if you are saved, you will be part of another wedding. This wedding will be the wedding of all weddings. There will be no expense spared. There will be no prenuptial agreement. There will be no cold feet. You will be surrounded by millions of people. There will be love in the air. There will be a chattering of people as everyone anticipates the arrival of the groom. There will be excitement, oh how there will be excitement! What am I talking about? I'm talking about the day that every born-again believer, every Christian, every person who has confessed their sins and committed their life to God is spiritually married to Jesus Christ, God's one and only Son. So let's walk down the aisle of the Bible as we study a marriage made for Heaven.

IS THIS MARRIAGE MENTIONED IN THE BIBLE?

Yes! It is mentioned in several places. Jesus refers to this marriage in two of His parables:

Matthew 22:1-14: Once more Jesus spoke to them in parables: "The kingdom of heaven may be compared to a king who gave a wedding banquet for his son. He sent out his slaves to summon those invited to the banquet, but they didn't want to come. Again, he sent out other slaves, and said, 'Tell those who are invited: Look, I've prepared my dinner; my oxen and fattened cattle have been slaughtered, and everything is ready. Come to the wedding banquet.' But they paid no attention and went away, one to his own farm, another to his business. And the others seized his slaves, treated them outrageously and killed them. The king was enraged, so he sent out his troops, destroyed those murderers, and burned down their city. Then he told his slaves, 'The banquet is ready, but those who were invited were not worthy. Therefore, go to where the roads exit the city and invite everyone you find to the banquet.' So those slaves went out on the roads and gathered everyone they found, both evil and good. The wedding banquet was filled with guests. But when the king came in to view the guests, he saw a man there who was not dressed for a wedding. So he said to him, 'Friend, how did you get in here without wedding clothes?' The man was speechless. Then the king told the attendants, 'Tie him up hand and foot, and throw him into the outer darkness, where there will be weeping and *gnashing of teeth.' For many are invited, but few are chosen.*

Matthew 25:1-13: *Then the kingdom of heaven will be like 10 virgins who took their lamps and went out to meet the groom. Five of them were foolish and five were sensible. When the foolish took their lamps, they didn't take oil with them. But the sensible ones took oil in their flasks with their lamps. Since the groom was delayed, they all became drowsy and fell asleep. In the middle of the night there was a shout: 'Here's the groom! Come out to meet him. Then all those virgins got up and trimmed their lamps. But the foolish ones said to the sensible ones, 'Give us some of your oil, because our lamps are going out.' The sensible ones answered, 'No, there won't be enough for us and for you. Go instead to those who sell, and buy oil for yourselves.'*

When they had gone to buy some, the groom arrived. Then those who were ready went in with him to the wedding banquet, and the door was shut. Later the rest of the virgins also came and said, 'Master, master, open up for us!' But he replied, 'I assure you: I do not know you!' Therefore be alert, because you don't know either the day or the hour.

Paul mentions the marriage in his writings:

Romans 7:4: *Therefore, my brothers, you also were put to death in relation to the law through the crucified body of the Messiah, so that you may belong to another—to Him who was raised from the dead—that we may bear fruit for God.*

2 Corinthians 11:2: *For I am jealous over you with a godly jealousy, because I have promised you in marriage to one husband—to present a pure virgin to Christ.*

Finally, John writes about the marriage celebration right before Jesus and the church return at the Second Coming:

Revelation 19:6-9: *Then I heard something like the voice of a vast multitude, like the sound of cascading waters, and like the rumbling of loud thunder, saying: Hallelujah—because our Lord God, the Almighty, has begun to reign! Let us be glad, rejoice, and give Him glory, because the marriage of the Lamb has come, and His wife has prepared herself. She was permitted to wear fine linen, bright and pure. For the fine linen represents the righteous acts of the saints. Then he said to me, "Write: Blessed are those invited to the marriage feast of the Lamb!" He also said to me, "These words of God are true."*

Where Does This Marriage Take Place?

When there is a marriage here on earth, the announcements are sent out and the place for the wedding is reserved. That place could be a church, a home, a beautiful garden, a gazebo, or a cruise ship. I've even heard of a wedding taking place at 2nd base of a softball field. That's where the couple actually met. He slid into 2nd base during a co-ed softball game, and she landed on top of him with a sprained ankle.

The symbolic marriage of the bride of Christ to Jesus, her groom, will take place in the place of all places: Heaven. We know that it takes place in Heaven because it is sandwiched between two events, the Judgment Seat of Christ and the Second Coming of Christ.

In Revelation 19:6-9, John records the marriage of the Lamb. The Greek interpretation of *"righteous acts of the saints"* is literally, *"the righteous saints."* From this we know the righteous saints will be given white linen to wear which represents their righteous actions. This white linen robe is given to them in Heaven, and then is worn as they follow behind Christ on white horses when He returns to the Earth at His Second Coming (Revelation 19:14).

Who Are the Participants In the Marriage?

The first participant is God, the Father. He is pictured as the king, who sends out His servants to the invited guests in the parable of the Great Banquet in Matthew 22:2: *"The kingdom of heaven may be compared to a king who gave a wedding banquet for his son."*

71

The second participant is Jesus, the Bridegroom. He is the groom mentioned in the parable of the Ten Virgins in Matthew 25:1-13.

John the Baptist calls Jesus the bridegroom in John 3:27-30: *"No one can receive a single thing unless it's given to him from heaven. You yourselves can testify that I said, 'I am not the Messiah, but I've been sent ahead of Him.' He who has the bride is the groom. But the groom's friend, who stands by and listens for him, rejoices greatly at the groom's voice. So this joy of mine is complete. He must increase, but I must decrease."* John the Baptist is the groom's friend, or best man.

Jesus calls Himself the Bridegroom in Luke 5:33-35: *"Then they said to Him, 'John's disciples fast often and say prayers, and those of the Pharisees do the same, but Yours eat and drink. Jesus said to them, 'You can't make the wedding guests fast while the groom is with them, can you? But the days will come when the groom will be taken away from them—then they will fast in those days.'"*

The third participant is believers of the New Testament church. As we have already seen, they are the bride dressed in a white linen robe. The apostle Paul writes about the bride in Ephesians 5:22-33. Pastors read this passage at wedding ceremonies because it is helpful to understand the biblical relationship between husbands and wives. But the context of this passage is about Christ's relationship with the church.

> *"Wives, submit to your own husbands as to the Lord, for the husband is head of the wife as also Christ is head of the church. He is the Savior of the body. Now as the church submits to Christ, so wives should submit to their husbands in everything. Husbands, love your wives, just as*

also Christ loved the church and gave Himself for her, to make her holy, cleansing her in the washing of water by the word. He did this to present the church to Himself in splendor, without spot or wrinkle or any such thing, but holy and blameless. In the same way, husbands should love their wives as their own bodies. He who loves his wife loves himself. For no one ever hates his own flesh, but provides and cares for it, just as Christ does for the church, since we are members of His body. For this reason a man will leave his father and mother and be joined to his wife, and the two will become one flesh. **This mystery is profound, but I am talking about Christ and the church.** *To sum up, each one of you is to love his wife as himself, and the wife is to respect her husband."* (emphasis added)

Let me take a moment and address what has become an issue in our modern culture. I'm talking about wives submitting to their husbands. Many bristle at the idea of a wife submitting to her husband like a second-class citizen. I can promise you Glynis wouldn't tolerate that for a second, nor would she overlook that type of treatment from me.

Here's what I believe Paul was really saying about the marriage relationship between a husband and a wife:

1. In any relationship there has to be a leader. Paul says the leader is the husband, just as Christ is the head of the church. I know that is not popular in our 21st century world, but it is biblical, and in my experience as a pastor and husband for 35 plus years, the

marriage relationship works best under this mutually accepted pattern.

2. The marriage relationship is built on mutual respect. Husbands are to love their wives and die for them if necessary, as Christ died for the church (v. 25), and wives are to love and respect their husbands (v. 33).

3. Husbands are to love their wives as their own bodies. A man protects, cares for, and nurtures his own body, and he should do the same for his wife. As Christ does for His church, a husband is to do for his wife.

4. Throughout the passage, Paul talks about the husband and wife giving to each other. The marriage relationship is about putting each other's needs before your own needs. Marriage is supposed to be the most unselfish relationship we have in our life, but, unfortunately, we've made it the most selfish relationship. My relationship with Christ is not about me, but about Him, and His relationship with me is not about Him, but about me; that's why He died on the cross for me. He sacrificed Himself for me, and I should follow His example and sacrifice myself for my wife; likewise she should do the same.

5. Our earthly marriage is to be a picture of our spiritual marriage to Jesus in Heaven. Marriage on Earth is supposed to give us a taste of what it will be like to be married to Jesus in eternity.

Paul goes on to say, *"For I am jealous over you with a godly jealousy, because I have promised you in marriage to one husband—to present a pure virgin to Christ"* (2 Corinthians 11:2).

It's crystal clear in the Bible that the Marriage of the Lamb is between Christ and believers of the New Testament church. So what about the Old Testament believers? Are they included in this marriage? Yes!

The fourth and final participants are the invited guests, and in my opinion, along with most Biblical scholars and theologians, the invited guests are three groups of believers.

The first group of invited guests is all Old Testament believers. These invited guests will be mostly Jews like Abraham and his sons, Moses, Joshua, Caleb, David, Solomon, and the prophets.

The second group of invited guests is all New Testament believers prior to the start of the church at Pentecost in Acts 2. These invited guests are mostly Jews like John the Baptist, Mary, Jesus' mother, Mary Magdalene, and many Jews Jesus healed during His public ministry.

The third group of invited guests will be the Tribulation saints. Pentecost (Acts 2) ushers in the New Testament church also called the Church Age or the Age of Grace. This age continues until the Rapture of the church. The believers saved during the Tribulation Period are not part of the New Testament church, but they are just as much saved as we are. Revelation 7 indicates there are 144,000 Jewish witnesses and the great multitude from every nation, tribe, people, and language standing before the Lamb. They are clothed in white robes, just as the raptured saints are. Revelation 7:13-17 tells us who they are:

> Then one of the elders asked me, "Who are these people robed in white, and where did they come from?" I said to him, "Sir, you know." Then he told me: "These are the ones coming

out of the great tribulation. They washed their robes and made them white in the blood of the Lamb. For this reason they are before the throne of God, and they serve Him day and night in His sanctuary. The One seated on the throne will shelter them: no longer will they hunger; no longer will they thirst; no longer will the sun strike them, or any heat. Because the Lamb who is at the center of the throne will shepherd them; He will guide them to springs of living waters, and God will wipe away every tear from their eyes."

These invited guests are those of the Great Tribulation (see the glossary or the next chapter) who were beheaded because of their testimony about Jesus and the Word of God, and because they did not worship the Beast or his image, and because they did not take the mark of the beast (666). They were resurrected to reign with Christ for 1,000 years.

Revelation 20:4: Then I saw thrones, and people seated on them who were given authority to judge. I also saw the souls of those who had been beheaded because of their testimony about Jesus and because of God's word, who had not worshiped the beast or his image, and who had not accepted the mark on their foreheads or their hands. They came to life and reigned with the Messiah for 1,000 years.

Is There A Biblical Pattern to the Marriage?

Yes! This marriage follows the pattern of a traditional New Testament Jewish wedding, which has three stages. The first stage is the marriage contract, also called the Betrothal Period. This is when the father of the groom and the father of the bride pledge their children to one another. From this point forward the bride is sanctified, or set apart exclusively for the groom. Matthew 1:18 says that Mary and Joseph were betrothed to one another: *"Now the birth of Jesus Christ was on this wise: When as his mother Mary was espoused to Joseph, before they came together, she was found with child of the Holy Ghost" (KJV).*

Once the bride and groom are pledged to one another, the father of the groom pays a dowry to the father of the bride. This payment of the dowry is connected with the church today. How? As we've discussed, Christian believers are the bride of Jesus and are in the marriage contract stage right now, having been promised to Jesus as his bride. Jesus left the home of His Father (Heaven) and traveled to the home of His promised bride (Earth) to purchase her by paying the dowry. What was the dowry that was paid by Jesus for His bride (the church)? It was His very own death on the cross. 1 Corinthians 6:19-20 says, *"Haven't you yet learned that your body is the home of the Holy Spirit God gave you, and that he lives within you? Your own body does not belong to you. For God has bought you with a great price. So use every part of your body to give glory back to God because he owns it" (TLB).*

The second part of the New Testament Jewish wedding is the claiming of the bride. This is where the groom, accompanied by male escorts, comes for his bride and takes her back to his father's house for a celebration. The exact time of his arrival was not usually known in advance, but was announced with a shout. This is illustrated in the Parable of the Ten Virgins in Matthew 25:1-13. This is what will happen when Jesus returns for the church at the Rapture.

As of today, the church has been set apart for her groom, Jesus, but one day He will come for her and take her away from the Earth (the Rapture) and return with her to His Father's house (Heaven). He will be accompanied by angelic escorts, and it will be preceded by a shout.

> *1 **Thessalonians 4:16-18:** For the Lord Himself will descend from heaven with a shout, with the archangel's voice, and with the trumpet of God, and the dead in Christ will rise first. Then we who are still alive will be caught up together with them in the clouds to meet the Lord in the air; and so we will always be with the Lord. Therefore encourage one another with these words.*

In the traditional Jewish wedding, the groom takes his bride to his father's house and keeps her there for seven days. After seven days he brings her out and reveals her to the community. In the marriage of the church to Jesus, He takes the church to His Father's house and keeps her for seven years (the Tribulation Period). After seven years Jesus brings out His bride and returns with her to the Earth in full view of the world. Colossians 3:4 says, *"When the Messiah, who is your life, is revealed, then you also will be revealed with Him in glory."*

The third phase of the New Testament Jewish wedding is the celebration stage. In the Bible this lasted seven days and was celebrated by the entire community. With regard to the church, this is the marriage supper of the Lamb and takes place on the Earth at the Second Coming of Jesus. This marriage supper involves the Father, Jesus, His bride, all invited guests, and now the remnant of Jews that fled to Petra when the anti-Christ relocated his world headquarters to Jerusalem during the last half of the Tribulation Period. These Jews are those who the servants invited to the king's banquet in Matthew 22:9-10, and the five wise virgins who were prepared for the groom and went into the wedding banquet in Matthew 25:10. Consequently, the original invited guests who were unworthy of the king's banquet in Matthew 22 and the five foolish virgins in Matthew 25 are the Jews who believe the anti-Christ is the Messiah and take the mark of the beast (666).

This marriage supper of the Lamb is an actual meal that Jesus will serve to us.

> **Luke 12:35-38:** *Keep your shirts on; keep the lights on! Be like house servants waiting for their master to come back from his honeymoon, awake and ready to open the door when he arrives and knocks. Lucky the servants whom the master finds on watch! He'll put on an apron, sit them at the table, and serve them a meal, sharing his wedding feast with them. (The Message)*

7 POINTS OF REVIEW:

1. The marriage is for believers only and takes place in Heaven, the home of God, the Father.

2. There are two primary participants in the marriage: Jesus and believers of the church.

3. Ephesians 5:22-33 is a passage that pastors often read at marriage ceremonies because it helps the bride and groom understand the relationship between the husband and wife. But the context of the passage is really about the relationship between Jesus and the church.

4. The marriage of the Lamb follows the pattern of a traditional Jewish wedding with three stages. The first stage is the marriage contract where the fathers of the groom and bride pledge their children to marry each other. The second stage is the claiming of the bride by the groom. The third stage is the celebration meal.

5. In the second stage of the marriage ceremony, the groom comes for the bride and takes her back to his father's house. The arrival is unknown but is announced with a shout. This is referred to in 1 Thessalonians 4:16-18 and illustrated in the Parable of the Ten Virgins in Matthew 25:1-15.

6. The third stage of the wedding celebration is the actual meal and takes place on the Earth at Jesus'

Second Coming, and it involves Israel as indicated in Matthew 22:1-14 and Matthew 25:1-13. Luke 12:35-37 indicates that Jesus, the groom, will actually serve the marriage supper to His bride, the church.

7. We are in the contract stage or the Betrothal stage of the ceremony right now, as Jesus has selected His bride (the church), paid the dowry by dying on the cross, and is now gone preparing a home for us in Heaven, as indicated by John 14:1-3.

5 BIG QUESTIONS:

1. In what Bible passages is the marriage mentioned? List them:

_____

_____

_____

2. The marriage is sandwiched between two events. What are those two events?

_____

_____

_____

3. What are the four points made by the Apostle Paul about the husband/wife relationship from Ephesians 5:22-33?

_____

_____

_____

4. As discussed in the chapter, who are the three groups of wedding guests who are invited to the marriage?

_____

_____

_____

5. What are the symbolic meanings between the groom and the bride in a Jewish marriage ceremony and Jesus and the New Testament church? List them here:

_____

_____

_____

CHAPTER 5

THE TRIBULATION PERIOD

For then there will be great tribulation (affliction, distress, and oppression) such as has not been from the beginning of the world until now—no, and never will be [again]. [Dan 12:1; Joel 2:2.] And if those days had not been shortened, no human being would endure and survive, but for the sake of the elect (God's chosen ones) those days will be shortened.
Matthew 24:21-22 (AMP)

In the Bible there are several names for the Tribulation Period:

- Indignation (Isaiah 26:20; 34:2)
- Day of God's Vengeance (Isaiah 34:8; 63:1-6)
- Time of Jacob's Trouble (Jeremiah 30:7)
- Overspread of Abomination (Daniel 9:27)
- Time of the End (Daniel 12:9)
- 70th Week (Daniel 9:24-27)
- Day of Trouble (Zephaniah 1:14-15)
- End of the World (Matthew 13:40-49)
- Tribulation (Matthew 24:29)
- Great Tribulation (Matthew 24:21)

- Great Day of His Wrath (Revelation 6:16-17)
- Hour of His Judgment (Revelation 14:7)

The Tribulation is a period on God's prophetic calendar that will happen soon after the Rapture. While Christians are in Heaven at the Judgment Seat of Christ and the Marriage of the Lamb, unbelievers will go through the seven years of Tribulation on the Earth.

WHAT IS THE PURPOSE OF THE TRIBULATION PERIOD?

The primary purpose is to prepare Israel for her Messiah. Zechariah and Malachi both prophesied that the Tribulation Period is a time of purifying Israel:

> *Zechariah 13:8-9:* In the whole land—the Lord's declaration—two-thirds will be cut off and die, but a third will be left in it. I will put this third through the fire; I will refine them as silver is refined and test them as gold is tested. They will call on My name, and I will answer them. I will say: They are My people, and they will say: The Lord is our God.

Jesus is Israel's purifier:

> *Malachi 3:3:* He will be like a refiner and purifier of silver; He will purify the sons of Levi (Israel) and refine them like gold and silver. Then they will present offerings to the Lord in righteousness.

The secondary purpose of the Tribulation Period is to pour out judgment on all unrighteousness on the Earth. Not only is it a time of purifying for Israel, but it is also a time of purifying for the entire Earth.

> **Isaiah 26:21:** *For look, the Lord is coming from His place to punish the inhabitants of the earth for their iniquity. The earth will reveal the blood shed on it and will no longer conceal her slain.*

> **Romans 1:18:** *For God's wrath is revealed from heaven against all godlessness and unrighteousness of people who by their unrighteousness suppress the truth...*

> **2 Thessalonians 2:11-12:** *For this reason God sends them a strong delusion so that they will believe what is false, so that all will be condemned—those who did not believe the truth but enjoyed unrighteousness.*

What is this delusion that God sends so the unrighteous will believe the lie? Note that the delusion comes from God to the inhabitants of the Earth. Since God cannot lie, the lie must come from the anti-Christ that rises to power at the beginning of the Tribulation Period. In my opinion, the lie refers to what happens to all those that suddenly disappeared from the Earth. We know the great disappearance as the Rapture of the church. What could this lie from the anti-Christ be? Again, in my opinion, I think the lie could be alien abduction. Now, this may sound silly, but don't completely dismiss my theory. Think about all the movies and TV shows that have some kind of alien abduction in the plot. For those of us old enough, we can go all the way back to "Close Encounters of the Third Kind." More recently there are the TV shows "4400" and "100."

Satan knows God is going to come one day for His church and, like you and I, he doesn't know when God will come. What better way to prepare the world for a great disappearance than to put into the minds of people now, that there are alien life forms out there who will come and take selected people from the Earth? Do I know for sure this will be the lie? No! But, I believe it is possible. As I teach this theory (and it's just a theory), I ask those in attendance, "What do you think the lie will be?" Every single time someone will say, "Alien abduction." Why do they say this? Because it has been planted in our minds through science fiction and entertainment.

WHAT ARE THE SIGNS THAT LEAD UP TO THE TRIBULATION PERIOD?

Matthew 24:1-8 reveals three signs leading up to the Tribulation: religious deception (vv. 4-5), wars and rumors of wars (vv. 6-7a), and natural disasters (v. 7b):

> *Matthew 24:1-8: As Jesus left and was going out of the temple complex, His disciples came up and called His attention to the temple buildings. Then He replied to them, "Don't you see all these things? I assure you: Not one stone will be left here on another that will not be thrown down!" While He was sitting on the Mount of Olives, the disciples approached Him privately and said, "Tell us, when will these*

things happen? And what is the sign of Your coming and of the end of the age?"

Then Jesus replied to them: "Watch out that no one deceives you. For many will come in My name, saying, 'I am the Messiah,' and they will deceive many. You are going to hear of wars and rumors of wars. See that you are not alarmed, because these things must take place, but the end is not yet. For nation will rise up against nation, and kingdom against kingdom. There will be famines and earthquakes in various places. All these events are the beginning of birth pains."

Leading up to the Tribulation Period there will be an increase in religious deception. I believe we are living in this time right now. There are a number of false religions that either claims their leader to be the returned Christ, or their version of the Bible to be from God. Any religion that does not acknowledge Jesus Christ as Messiah, Savior, or Almighty God, and any religion that does not acknowledge the Holy Bible as the true and only Word from God, is a false religion. There are some denominations that have their own additions to the Bible. There is only one Holy Bible and it comes straight from God, the Father. It is the Word of God and it is the Word in the flesh (John 1:14).

What is meant by "rumors of wars?" I believe it could be the war on global terrorism. It wears no uniform, it doesn't have a national flag, and it puts fear in the lives of innocent people. In Israel and other parts of the world, you cannot walk down the street without wondering if the person you just passed has a bomb strapped to his chest. One may also sit in a restaurant thinking at any moment someone could walk in and detonate an IED. Imagine looking intently at everyone around you to see if they have a bomb underneath their coat. That's a "rumor of war."

We have seen an increase in natural disasters around the world. Of the ten deadliest tornadoes in the United States, half have happened in the last 100 years. Twenty of the thirty deadliest hurricanes in the USA have occurred since 1900.

Just as Matthew records signs leading up to the Tribulation Period, he gives us three signs that will happen during the Tribulation Period:

> *Matt 24:9-14: Then they will hand you over for persecution, and they will kill you. You will be hated by all nations because of My name. Then many will take offense, betray one another and hate one another. Many false prophets will rise up and deceive many. Because lawlessness will multiply, the love of many will grow cold. But the one who endures to the end will be delivered. This good news of the kingdom will be proclaimed in all the world as a testimony to all nations. And then the end will come.*

1. Believers will be handed over to be persecuted (v. 9).
2. Defection of false believers from Christ (vv. 10-13).
3. Declaration of the Good News to the world (v. 14).

Jesus said those saved during the Tribulation Period (yes, there will be people saved during the Tribulation) will be delivered up, persecuted, and killed because of their faith in Jesus. Right now, the Holy Spirit is holding back the full work of Satan and his unholy trinity (2 Thessalonians 2:6-7). When the Holy Spirit departs with the church at the Rapture, the anti-Christ will be unleashed on the Earth. There will be no presence of God to restrain him. His full wickedness and evil will have free reign for the first time on the Earth.

Jesus goes on to say there will be a defection of false believers from Christ. They are ones that pretend to be of God, but their real intent is to lead people away from God. They are false believers because:

1. They turn away from Jesus and betray their family and friends (v. 10). They will be characterized as haters because when they betray their family and friends, they won't think twice about it.
2. They will believe the deception of many false prophets (v. 11). These false prophets will be very convincing.
3. They become cold and wicked (v. 12). They will flaunt their sin in public and this will lure others into their wickedness.

The third sign of the Tribulation Period that Jesus gives will be a declaration of the Good News to the world (v. 14). Even in the worst of times, God is still calling sinners to faith.

WHO ARE THE EVANGELISTS WHO DECLARE THE GOOD NEWS TO THE WORLD?

We find them mentioned in two places:

Revelation 7:2-8: Then I saw another angel rise up from the east, who had the seal of the living God. He cried out in a loud voice to the four angels who were empowered to harm the earth and the sea: "Don't harm the earth or the sea or the trees until we seal the slaves of our God on their foreheads." And I heard the number of those who were sealed:

144,000 sealed from every tribe of the sons of Israel:
12,000 sealed from the tribe of Judah,
12,000 from the tribe of Reuben,
12,000 from the tribe of Gad,
12,000 from the tribe of Asher,
12,000 from the tribe of Naphtali,
12,000 from the tribe of Manasseh,
12,000 from the tribe of Simeon,
12,000 from the tribe of Levi,
12,000 from the tribe of Issachar,
12,000 from the tribe of Zebulun,
12,000 from the tribe of Joseph,
12,000 sealed from the tribe of Benjamin.

Revelation 14:1-5: *Then I looked, and there on Mount Zion stood the Lamb, and with Him were 144,000 who had His name and His Father's name written on their foreheads. I heard a sound from heaven like the sound of cascading waters and like the rumbling of loud thunder. The sound I heard was also like harpists playing on their harps. They sang a new song before the throne and before the four living creatures and the elders, but no one could learn the song except the 144,000 who had been redeemed from the earth. These are the ones not defiled with women, for they have kept their virginity. These are the ones who follow the Lamb* *wherever He goes. They were redeemed from the human race as the firstfruits for God and the Lamb. No lie was found in their mouths; they are blameless.*

Here's what the Bible reveals about them:

- They are 144,000 Jews, 12,000 from each of the 12 tribes of Israel (Revelation 7:4-8).
- They are servants of God and they are sealed by God on their foreheads (Revelation 7:3).
- They are pure, unmarried virgin men totally committed to God (Revelation 14:4).
- They are sealed by God as the firstfruits (Revelation 14:4).
- They have a special mission (Matthew 24:14) and are called to evangelize the post-Rapture world and proclaim the gospel during the Tribulation Period before Christ's Second Coming.
- They get the job done (Revelation 7:9, 13-14). Many people are saved because of the success of the Jewish evangelists.
- They have a special place in Heaven at the throne of God. They have a song that only they sing because they have been redeemed from the Earth (Revelation 14:3).

The message the 144,000 evangelists preach is the message of the three angels found in Revelation 14:6-12. The first angel said to fear God, give Him glory, and worship the One who created everything. The second angel tells of the fall of Satan's kingdom. The third angel said to those who take the mark of the beast (666) they will be tormented day and night and there will be no rest for them.

What Does The Bible Reveal About The Mark Of The Tribulation Period?

> *Revelation 13:16-18: And he requires everyone— small and great, rich and poor, free and slave— to be given a mark on his right hand or on his forehead, so that no one can buy or sell unless he has the mark: the beast's name or the number of his name. Here is wisdom: The one who has understanding must calculate the number of the beast, because it is the number of a man. His number is 666.*

- It is the number of man. Many believe the number of completion, or the number of God, is "7," and a reference to the six days of creation, with God resting on the seventh day. The number "6" is one number short of completion, or one number short of God, so it is the number of man.
- During the Tribulation Period, people will be required to have the mark to buy or sell anything necessary to live.
- This mark will either be on the right hand or on the forehead.
- This mark could be visible or invisible. Some have raised the possibility that it could be an ultra-violet mark, or some kind of implanted microchip.
- This mark is forced on people by the False Prophet to show one's allegiance to the anti-Christ.

- This mark will bring God's wrath on the persons who receive it (Revelation 16:2).
- This mark is irrevocable. Once it is taken, it seals a person's future (Revelation 14:9-11).
- The "666" represents the unholy trinity. Just as there is a Holy Trinity (Father, Son, and Holy Spirit), there is an unholy trinity (Satan, anti-Christ, False Prophet).

WHO ARE THE TWO WITNESSES OF THE TRIBULATION PERIOD?

Revelation 11:1-14: Then I was given a measuring reed like a rod, with these words: "Go and measure God's sanctuary and the altar, and count those who worship there. But exclude the courtyard outside the sanctuary. Don't measure it, because it is given to the nations, and they will trample the holy city for 42 months. I will empower my two witnesses, and they will prophesy for 1,260 days, dressed in sackcloth." These are the two olive trees and the two lampstands that stand before the Lord of the earth. If anyone wants to harm them, fire comes from their mouths and consumes their enemies; if anyone wants to harm them, he must be killed in this way. These men have the power to close the sky so that it does not rain during the days of their prophecy. They also have power over the waters to turn them into blood, and to strike the earth with any plague whenever they want.

When they finish their testimony, the beast that comes up out of the abyss will make war with them, conquer them, and kill them. Their dead bodies will lie in the public square of the great city, which is called, prophetically, Sodom and Egypt, where also their Lord was crucified. And representatives from the peoples, tribes, languages, and nations will view their bodies for three and a half days and not permit their bodies to be put into a tomb. Those who live on the earth will gloat over them and celebrate and send gifts to one another, because these two prophets tormented those who live on the earth.

But after the three and a half days, the breath of life from God entered them, and they stood on their feet. So great fear fell on those who saw them. Then they heard a loud voice from heaven saying to them, "Come up here." They went up to heaven in a cloud, while their enemies watched them. At that moment a violent earthquake took place, a tenth of the city fell, and 7,000 people were killed in the earthquake. The survivors were terrified and gave glory to the God of heaven. The second woe has passed. Take note: the third woe is coming quickly!

There are three theories regarding the identity of the two witnesses. The first theory says they are Moses and Elijah because their miracles are identical to the miracles of the two witnesses. They have the power to destroy people with fire; that's Elijah's miracle in 2 Kings 1. They have the authority to withhold rain on the Earth; that's Elijah's miracle in 1 Kings 17:1. They have the power to turn the water to blood; that's Moses' miracle in Exodus 7:14-24. They have the power to strike the Earth with plagues; that's Moses' miracle in Exodus 7-11.

The second theory says the two witnesses are Elijah and Enoch because both were taken to Heaven and did not experience death (Genesis 5:23-24; 2 Kings 2:11). Many believe since Elijah and Enoch have not died, this qualifies them to be the two witnesses who die and then are resurrected three days later. Proponents of this theory believe Moses is disqualified because he already died once (Deuteronomy 34:5). But there are several people in the Bible who died twice, Lazarus being the most famous (John 11), but also Dorcas (Acts 9:36-42), and the synagogue ruler's daughter (Luke 8:49-56), so Moses should not be disqualified based on his death.

The third theory claims the two witnesses are not necessarily famous, that God has the ability to raise up two unknown believers and enable them to preach and perform the miracles.

While there is nothing in Revelation 11 that indicates who the two witnesses are, I lean toward Moses and Elijah, because of their miracles, and because both appeared with Jesus at the Transfiguration (Matthew 17:1-13).

The truth is no one knows for sure who the two witnesses will be, but the Bible does give us a lot of information about them:

- They have special powers (Revelation 11:5-6).
- They have a limited time to prophesy during the Tribulation Period – 1,260 days or 3.5 years (Revelation 11:3).
- They have a special message (Revelation 11:4). John records they are two olive trees that stand before the Lord on the Earth. In the Bible, an olive tree or olive branch is a symbol of peace and new life. After the flood, the dove returned to Noah with an olive branch signaling the waters had receded and new life had started. The two witnesses are extending the peace of God even during the worst time the Earth has ever experienced.
- John also says the two witnesses are two lampstands. He records in Revelation 1:12-13 that he saw seven golden lampstands and Christ standing in the middle of them. Symbolically, the lampstand is the light that points directly to Christ. As the church, we are to walk in the light of Christ (1 John 1:7) and spread the light of God's message so the world will come to God. The two witnesses are spreading the light that points to Jesus, the true Savior of the world, even during the Tribulation Period.
- They get no respect from the people (Revelation 11:8-10). Their deaths are celebrated by gloating over them and sending gifts to one another.
- They have a big surprise for the people when their bodies are resurrected and called up to Heaven (Revelation 11:11-12).
- They appear shortly after the Rapture and are instrumental in sending the 144,000 Jewish evangelists into the world.

WHAT ARE THE EVENTS OF THE TRIBULATION AND WHAT IS THE GREAT TRIBULATION?

There are three parts to the Tribulation Period. The first three and a half years will be peaceful and many will believe the anti-Christ to be the Messiah. Then there is the middle of the Tribulation Period, which will be about two weeks in length. The final three and a half years is called the Great Tribulation because all hell is unleashed on the Jews and the people of the world.

Here are the major events of the Tribulation Period divided into the three time periods:

First 3.5 years of the Tribulation Period:

- The appearance of the anti-Christ and the False Prophet (Daniel 7:19-25).
- Organization of the one-world church (Revelation 13).
- The organizing of the old Roman Empire into a 10-nation federation (Daniel 2:40-44, 7:7-8; Revelation 13:1, 17:7, 12).
- The anti-Christ signs a 7-year treaty with Israel (Daniel 9:27).
- The appearance of the two witnesses sent by God (Revelation 11:1-6).
- The rebuilding of the temple in Jerusalem (Revelation 11:1-2).
- The 1st Seal Judgment is opened (Revelation 6:1-2). The rider on the white horse is the anti-Christ. He has words of peace.

Middle of the Tribulation Period (probably a two-week period):

- The battle of Gog and Magog (Ezekiel 38-39). This is the Islamic invasion of Israel by a coalition of nations led by Russia, Iran, Iraq, and Muslim African nations.
- The treaty between Israel and the anti-Christ is broken (Daniel 9:27). This is the 2nd Seal Judgment (Revelation 6:3-4). After this, Seals 3-6 are opened in succession.
- The two witnesses of God are killed. Their bodies lay in the street for three and a half days, and then they are resurrected to life and ascend into Heaven (Revelation 11:1-14).
- The 144,000 Jewish evangelists could possibly be killed. Some Bible scholars believe they will live through the Tribulation Period.

Last 3.5 years of the Tribulation Period (The Great Tribulation):

- The full and complete manifestation of the anti-Christ is poured out on the Earth. He will unleash all of his evil, wickedness, and unrighteousness on the people of the Earth (Matthew 24:21-22; Jeremiah 30:5-7; Zechariah 14:1-2).
- He will move his world headquarters from Babylon to Jerusalem.
- He goes into the temple and sets himself up as God. The False Prophet makes a statue of the anti-Christ, puts it in the Holy of Holies, and makes it speak (Matthew 24:14; Daniel 9:27, 12:11; 2 Thessalonians

2:4). This leads to worldwide religious confusion (Matthew 24:22-27).

- The pouring out of the 7th Seal Judgment and the start of the 7 Trumpet Judgments (Revelation 8:1-9:21, 11:15-19).
- Satan is banned from Heaven and tries to destroy Israel (Revelation 12).
- The Jews flee Israel (Matthew 24:15-20). Most Jews follow the anti-Christ, but some will flee to the land called Petra or Edom (Revelation 12:14).
- The message of the three angels (Revelation 14:6-13).
- The mark of the beast (666) will be administered (Revelation 13:16-18).
- The final 7 Bowl Judgments are poured out on the Earth (Revelation 15-16).
- The world will become spiritually dead (Matthew 24:28).

WHAT ARE THE JUDGMENTS OF THE TRIBULATION PERIOD?

During the Tribulation chapters (Revelation 6-19), John records twenty-one judgments of God on the Earth. They are the Seal Judgments in Revelation 6, the Trumpet Judgments in Revelation 8, and Bowl Judgments in Revelation 16. Let's look in detail at God's judgments of the Tribulation Period.

THE SEAL JUDGMENTS

FIRST SEAL:

The first four Seal Judgments give us the "The Four Horsemen of The Apocalypse." It's possible that the four horsemen are symbolic of peace, war, famine, and death; but I lean to believe they are actual riders, and if they are, then I believe the four riders are in fact, the same rider, the anti-Christ.

> **Revelation 6:1-2:** *Then I saw the Lamb open one of the seven seals, and I heard one of the four living creatures say with a voice like thunder, "Come!" I looked, and there was a white horse. The horseman on it had a bow; a crown was given to him, and he went out as a victor to conquer.*

[White Horse—PEACE]: This Seal is opened about a week after the Rapture. Do not confuse this rider with Christ, the rider of the white horse in Revelation 19:11-14. This rider is the anti-Christ. There are three reasons why:

1. It's the beginning of the Tribulation Period. Christ is in Heaven with the raptured church going through the Judgment Seat of Christ and the Marriage to the Lamb.
2. The other 3 horsemen bring war, famine, and death.
3. The anti-Christ is a copycat, a Christ-imitator. During the first half of the Tribulation Period, he represents himself as good, and many people believe him to be the Messiah. Notice, he carries a bow with no arrows. The first half of the Tribulation Period is a time of peace on the Earth.

Note: Some Bible scholars believe the second Seal Judgment is not opened until the middle of the Tribulation Period, and ushers in the "Great Tribulation." That means there is a 3.5-year gap between the opening of the first and second seals.

SECOND SEAL:

> *Revelation 6:3-4:* When He opened the second seal, I heard the second living creature say, "Come!" Then another horse went out, a fiery red one, and its horseman was empowered to take peace from the earth, so that people would slaughter one another. And a large sword was given to him.

[Red Horse—WAR]: The anti-Christ has the power to take away peace from the Earth. There is tremendous blood shed during this time. The anti-Christ goes from carrying a bow to carrying a sword.

THIRD SEAL:

> *Revelation 6:5-6:* When He opened the third seal, I heard the third living creature say, "Come!" And I looked, and there was a black horse. The horseman on it had a balance scale in his hand. Then I heard something like a voice among the four living creatures say, "A quart of wheat for a denarius, and three quarts of barley for a denarius—but do not harm the olive oil and the wine."

[Black Horse—FAMINE]: Food will get very expensive. It will take a full day's wage to buy one quart of wheat. The rich will get richer, the poor will get poorer, and middle class will disappear.

FOURTH SEAL:

> *Revelation 6:7-8:* When He opened the fourth seal, I heard the voice of the fourth living creature say, "Come!" And I looked, and there was a pale green horse. The horseman on it was named Death, and Hades was following after him. Authority was given to them over a fourth of the earth, to kill by the sword, by famine, by plague, and by the wild animals of the earth.

[Pale Horse—DEATH]: A fourth of the Earth's population will die by sword, hunger, and disease.

Let's say for the sake of argument the Earth's population at the opening time of the fourth Seal Judgment is 10 billion, and one billion Christians are raptured just before the start of the Tribulation Period. That leaves the Earth's population at 9 billion. At the opening of the fourth Seal, a fourth of the Earth's population dies, that's 2.25 billion. This leaves the population at 6.75 billion. Keep this in mind when we get to the sixth Trumpet Judgment.

FIFTH SEAL:

> *Revelation 6:9-11:* When He opened the fifth seal, I saw under the altar the souls of those slaughtered because of God's word and the testimony they had. They cried out with a loud voice: "O Lord, holy and true, how long until

You judge and avenge our blood from those who live on the earth?" So a white robe was given to each of them, and they were told to rest a little while longer until the number of their fellow slaves and their brothers, who were going to be killed just as they had been, would be completed.

[MARTYRS]: The mark of the beast (666) is administered at the beginning of the Great Tribulation. There will be those that believe the message of the 144,000 Jewish evangelists, and see the anti-Christ for who he really is. They will refuse to take the mark, and by doing so they are killed, probably beheaded. According to vv. 10-11, these martyrs are believers and are given a white robe and brought to Heaven to rest until their fellow servants are killed.

SIXTH SEAL:

Revelation 6:12-17: Then I saw Him open the sixth seal. A violent earthquake occurred; the sun turned black like sackcloth made of goat hair; the entire moon became like blood; the stars of heaven fell to the earth as a fig tree drops its unripe figs when shaken by a high wind; the sky separated like a scroll being rolled up; and every mountain and island was moved from its place. Then the kings of the earth, the nobles, the military commanders, the rich, the powerful, and every slave and free person hid in the caves and among the rocks of the mountains. And they said to the mountains and to the rocks, "Fall on us and hide us from the face of the One seated on the throne and from the wrath of the Lamb, because the great day of Their wrath has come! And who is able to stand?"

[CHANGES TO THE EARTH]: Seven catastrophic events:

1. Earthquake
2. Sun turns black
3. Moon turns red
4. Stars fall from the sky
5. Sky separated
6. Every mountain and island is moved from its place.
7. People run to the mountains to hide from God.

SEVENTH SEAL:

Revelation 8:1-6: When He opened the seventh seal, there was silence in heaven for about half an hour. Then I saw the seven angels who stand in the presence of God; seven trumpets were given to them. Another angel, with a gold incense burner, came and stood at the altar. He was given a large amount of incense to offer with the prayers of all the saints on the gold altar in front of the throne. The smoke of the incense, with the prayers of the saints, went up in the presence of God from the angel's hand. The angel took the incense burner, filled it with fire from the altar, and hurled it to the earth; there were thunders, rumblings, lightnings, and an earthquake. And the seven angels who had the seven trumpets prepared to blow them.

[SEVEN TRUMPET JUDGEMENTS]: Out of the seventh Seal unfold the seven Trumpet Judgments. Why is there silence in Heaven? Four possible reasons:

1. The people of Heaven are in shock because there are seven more judgments.
2. The people of Heaven are waiting for the Trumpet Judgments to begin.
3. The people of Heaven are waiting to see what God does next.
4. The people of Heaven are praying (vv. 3-5).

THE TRUMPET JUDGMENTS

The Trumpet Judgments are poured out on the Earth over months. The first four Trumpets are directed toward nature. The last three Trumpets are directed toward humanity.

FIRST TRUMPET:

Revelation 8:7: The first angel blew his trumpet, and hail and fire, mixed with blood, were hurled to the earth. So a third of the earth was burned up, a third of the trees were burned up, and all the green grass was burned up.

These fiery balls hurled from Heaven are reminiscent of the fire from Heaven on the perverse cities of Sodom and Gomorrah (Genesis 19).

SECOND TRUMPET:

Revelation 8:8-9: The second angel blew his trumpet, and something like a great mountain ablaze with fire was hurled into the sea. So a third of the sea became blood, a third of the living creatures in the sea died, and a third of the ships were destroyed.

This judgment is on salt water. The seas and oceans are turned into blood, killing one third of all sea life and destroying one third of all sailing ships.

THIRD TRUMPET:

Revelation 8:10-11: The third angel blew his trumpet, and a great star, blazing like a torch, fell from heaven. It fell on a third of the rivers and springs of water. The name of the star is Wormwood, and a third of the waters became wormwood. So, many of the people died from the waters, because they had been made bitter.

This judgment is on fresh water. The fresh water becomes so bitter that it is unfit to drink. This Wormwood star could possibly be a meteor.

FOURTH TRUMPET:

Revelation 8:12-13: The fourth angel blew his trumpet, and a third of the sun was struck, a third of the moon, and a third of the stars, so that a third of them were darkened. A third of the day was without light, and the night as well. I looked, and I heard an eagle, flying in mid-heaven, saying in a loud voice, "Woe! Woe! Woe to those who live on the earth, because of the remaining trumpet blasts that the three angels are about to sound!"

The fourth trumpet affects the natural lights that illuminate the Earth. A third of the sun, moon, and stars are darkened. Daytime will seem like dusk, and night will be almost pitch black.

FIFTH TRUMPET:

Revelation 9:1-12: The fifth angel blew his trumpet, and I saw a star that had fallen from heaven to earth. The key to the shaft of the abyss was given to him. He opened the shaft of the abyss, and smoke came up out of the shaft like smoke from a great furnace so that the sun and the air were darkened by the smoke from the shaft. Then out of the smoke locusts came to the earth, and power was given to them like the power that scorpions have on the earth. They were told not to harm the grass of the earth, or any green plant, or any tree, but only people who do not have God's seal on their foreheads. They were not permitted to kill them, but were to torment them for five months; their torment is like the torment caused by a scorpion when it strikes a man. In those days people will seek death and will not find it; they will long to die, but death will flee from them.

The appearance of the locusts was like horses equipped for battle. On their heads were something like gold crowns; their faces were like men's faces; they had hair like women's hair; their teeth were like lions' teeth; they had chests like iron breastplates; the sound of their wings was like the sound of chariots with many horses rushing into battle; and they had tails with stingers, like scorpions, so that with their tails they had the power to harm people for five months. They had as their king the angel of the abyss; his name in Hebrew is Abaddon, and in Greek he has the name Apollyon. The first woe has passed. There are still two more woes to come after this.

The pit of Hell is opened, and horse-like locusts are released on the Earth. Their targets are those who have the mark of the beast (666). These locusts have the ability to sting people resulting in great suffering and torment for five months. Those stung will want to die, even attempt suicide, but they will not be able to achieve death.

SIXTH TRUMPET:

Revelation 9:13-21: The sixth angel blew his trumpet. From the four horns of the gold altar that is before God, I heard a voice say to the sixth angel who had the trumpet, "Release the four angels bound at the great river Euphrates." So the four angels who were prepared for the hour, day, month, and year were released to kill a third of the human race. The number of mounted troops was 200 million; I heard their number. This is how I saw the horses in my vision: The horsemen had breastplates that were fiery red, hyacinth blue, and sulfur yellow. The heads of the horses were like lions' heads, and from their mouths came fire, smoke, and sulfur. A third of the human race was killed by these three plagues—by the fire, the smoke, and the sulfur that came from their mouths. For the power of the horses is in their mouths and in their tails, because their tails, like snakes, have heads, and they inflict injury with them.

The rest of the people, who were not killed by these plagues, did not repent of the works of their hands to stop worshiping demons and idols of gold, silver, bronze, stone, and wood, which are not able to see, hear, or walk. And they did not repent of their murders, their sorceries, their sexual immorality, or their thefts.

An army of 200 million led by four demonic angels kill a third of the world's population by the plagues of fire, smoke, and sulfur. Those killed do not repent of their murders, sorceries, immoralities, or thefts.

Before the fourth Seal Judgment, I mentioned for the sake of argument that the Earth's population after the Rapture was at 9.0 billion, and then a fourth of the population was killed, leaving the Earth's population at 6.75 billion. Now at the sixth Trumpet Judgment, another third of the Earth's population is killed which is 2.23 billion. 6.75 billion – 2.23 = 4.52 billion.

My point is to show you that during the Tribulation Period the Earth's population will be cut in half. One out of two people on the Earth will die in seven years. How would the world be able to dispose of that many bodies? I don't believe it could. So that brings up a second question: What would the world smell like if there were rotting and decaying bodies everywhere? The smell would be atrocious. There would be nowhere you could go to get a breath of fresh air.

If you are reading this and you are an unbeliever, then realize you have a 50 percent chance of surviving the Tribulation Period, the worst time the world will ever see. When you go to work tomorrow, glance around the room at your office and say to yourself, "One out of two of us will die before Jesus returns at His Second Coming." One of those two could be you, or someone you love very much.

SEVENTH TRUMPET:

> *Revelation 11:15-19: The seventh angel blew his trumpet, and there were loud voices in heaven saying: The kingdom of the world has become the kingdom of our Lord and of His Messiah, and He will reign forever and ever! The 24 elders, who were seated before God on their thrones, fell on their faces and worshiped God, saying: We thank You, Lord God, the Almighty, who is and who was, because You have taken Your great power and have begun to reign. The nations were angry, but Your wrath has come.*

The time has come for the dead to be judged, and to give the reward to Your servants the prophets, to the saints, and to those who fear Your name, both small and great, and the time has come to destroy those who destroy the earth. God's sanctuary in heaven was opened, and the ark of His covenant appeared in His sanctuary. There were lightnings, rumblings, thunders, an earthquake, and severe hail.

This Trumpet announces the coming kingdom of Christ.

THE BOWL JUDGMENTS

The Bowl Judgments are the most severe of the judgments and are poured out on the Earth over the course of days.

FIRST BOWL:

Revelation 16:1-2: Then I heard a loud voice from the sanctuary saying to the seven angels, "Go and pour out the seven bowls of God's wrath on the earth." The first went and poured out his bowl on the earth, and severely painful sores broke out on the people who had the mark of the beast and who worshiped his image.

This is the judgment of God on those who have taken the mark of the beast (666). These sores will be unlike any sores we know about. They could be comparable to the sores on the Egyptians during Moses' plagues in the Old Testament (Exodus 9).

SECOND BOWL:

> *Revelation 16:3:* The second poured out his bowl into the sea. It turned to blood like a dead man's, and all life in the sea died.

During the 2nd Trumpet Judgment, a third of sea life was killed. Now all sea life is killed. The entire salt-water seas and oceans turn to blood, and all marine life will die.

THIRD BOWL:

> *Revelation 16:4-7:* The third poured out his bowl into the rivers and the springs of water, and they became blood. I heard the angel of the waters say: You are righteous, who is and who was, the Holy One, for You have decided these things. Because they poured out the blood of the saints and the prophets, You also gave them blood to drink; they deserve it! Then I heard someone from the altar say: Yes, Lord God, the Almighty, true and righteous are Your judgments.

In the 3rd Trumpet Judgment, a third of all fresh water contained in the rivers, lakes, and springs are made bitter and unfit to drink. Now all fresh water is unfit to drink.

FOURTH BOWL:

> *Revelation 16:8-9:* The fourth poured out his bowl on the sun. He was given the power to burn people with fire, and people were burned

by the intense heat. So they blasphemed the name of God who had the power over these plagues, and they did not repent and give Him glory.

The heat is turned up. People are sunburned beyond comprehension. No matter how bad it is, they will not repent. In fact, they do the opposite and curse God.

FIFTH BOWL:

Revelation 16:10-11: The fifth poured out his bowl on the throne of the beast, and his kingdom was plunged into darkness. People gnawed their tongues from pain and blasphemed the God of heaven because of their pains and their sores, yet they did not repent of their actions.

This plague is on the anti-Christ's ungodly leaders. Because of their pain they literally chew their own tongues, but get no relief. They refuse to repent.

Note: The sixth and seventh Bowl Judgments are part of the Second Coming of Jesus.

SIXTH BOWL:

Revelation 16:12-16: The sixth poured out his bowl on the great river Euphrates, and its water was dried up to prepare the way for the kings from the east. Then I saw three unclean spirits like frogs coming from the dragon's mouth, from the beast's mouth, and from the mouth of the false prophet. For they are spirits of demons performing signs, who travel to the kings of the whole world to assemble them for the battle of the great day of God, the Almighty. "Look, I am coming like a thief. Blessed is the one who is alert and remains clothed so that he may not go naked, and they see his shame." So they assembled them at the place called in Hebrew Armageddon.

The Euphrates River (located in present-day Iraq) is dried up, so the kings of the Earth and their armies can cross over to Armageddon. Unclean spirits come from the mouths of the unholy trinity (Satan, anti-Christ, and the False Prophet) and travel throughout the world, assembling an army for the Battle of Armageddon. This happens right before Jesus bursts on the scene at His Second Coming.

SEVENTH BOWL:

Revelation 16:17-21: Then the seventh poured out his bowl into the air, and a loud voice came out of the sanctuary, from the throne, saying, "It is done!" There were lightnings, rumblings, and thunders. And a severe earthquake occurred like no other since man has been on the earth—so great was the quake. The great city split into three parts, and the cities of the nations fell. Babylon the Great was remembered in God's presence; He gave her the cup filled with the wine of His fierce anger. Every island fled, and the mountains disappeared.

Enormous hailstones, each weighing about 100 pounds, fell from heaven on the people, and they blasphemed God for the plague of hail because that plague was extremely severe.

This is final judgment. A worldwide earthquake brings complete devastation to Jerusalem and all cities. Every island sinks, and every mountain collapses. God judges Satan, and huge hailstones fall from Heaven on the people of the Earth. They curse God because of the severity of the plagues. This brings to a close the worst period in human history and world history.

ARE PEOPLE SAVED DURING THE TRIBULATION PERIOD?

YES! Some believe there is no chance for salvation after the Rapture, but there is nothing in the Bible that says this is true. In fact, there is ample evidence from Scripture that reveals people do become believers after the Rapture, during the Tribulation Period.

1. In Revelation 6:9-11, at the opening of the fifth Seal Judgment, John saw the souls of those martyred because of their faith in the Word of God. They received a white robe just as the church did when it was raptured. If no one can be saved during the Tribulation Period, then why are people being martyred for their faith?

2. In Revelation 7:3-4, the 144,000 Jewish evangelists are believers who have the seal of God on their foreheads.

3. In Revelation 7:14-17, those coming out of the Great Tribulation washed their white robes in the blood of the Lamb (Jesus). They are before the throne of God day and night, and the One seated on the throne will provide and protect them. The Lamb, who is at the center of the throne, shepherds them, guides them, and wipes away every tear from their eyes.

4. In Revelation 9:4, the locusts are told to sting only those who do not have the seal of God on their foreheads. Who are those who have the seal of God? Believers of the Tribulation Period protected by God.

5. In Revelation 13:7, the Beast was given power to make war with the saints (believers). Since the church was raptured before the Tribulation Period, these saints must come to Christ during the Tribulation Period. Some say these saints are the Jews. While I do believe many Jews will be saved during the Tribulation Period, I do not believe the Jewish nation of Israel, as a whole, will acknowledge Jesus as the true Messiah until the Second Coming.

6. Revelation 14:13 presents a beatitude: *"Blessed are the dead who die in the Lord from now on."* The dead must refer to believers who die during the Tribulation Period. The Holy Spirit says they will rest from their labors and their deeds will follow them.

7. In Revelation 16:9, as the 4th angel pours out his bowl on the sun, people are scorched with intense heat, but they refuse to repent and glorify God. This emphasizes how those scorched had the ability to repent, indicating there are people who do repent during the Tribulation Period.

8. In Revelation 17:6, there are people who are referred to as saints and witnesses of Jesus, martyred by the woman (Satan).

9. In Revelation 20:1-6, Satan is bound and thrown into the abyss for 1,000 years. Verse 4 refers to the souls of those beheaded because of their testimony about Jesus and because of the Word of God. They did not worship the Beast, and they did not accept the mark (666) on their foreheads or right hands. They are resurrected to life and reign with Jesus for 1,000 years.

WHO ARE THE TRIBULATION SAINTS?

During the Tribulation Period, the anti-Christ, who is a counterfeit of Jesus, rules over the world. He is a lawless man, but has the ability to bring the world together for a time of peace and prosperity. He will accomplish what no world ruler before him has been able to do—bring total unity to the world. He will come to power at the beginning of the Tribulation Period, and he will be a military, economic, and religious genius. He will have all the answers to all the world's problems, and he will establish himself as the true world leader. During the first half of the Tribulation Period, the world will live in peace and harmony. Billions of people will see him as the Messiah and even worship him as the Savior. The anti-Christ will accept their worship to the point that he will demand their allegiance (Revelation 13:16-17).

Those who refuse to worship him are the Tribulation saints. The anti-Christ is permitted to wage war against them and even to conquer them, but their salvation is secure (Revelation 14:13). These saints are not silent during this time of Great Tribulation. They are faithful to the end and are rewarded by God:

> *Revelation 7:13-17: Then one of the elders asked me, "Who are these people robed in white, and where did they come from?" I said to him, "Sir, you know." Then he told me: These are the ones coming out of the great tribulation. They washed their robes and made them white in the blood of the Lamb. For this reason they are before the throne of God, and they serve Him day and night in His sanctuary. The One seated on the throne will shelter them: no longer will they hunger; no longer will they thirst; no longer will the sun strike them, or any heat. Because the Lamb who is at the center of the throne will shepherd them; He will guide them to springs of living waters, and God will wipe away every tear from their eyes.*

WHY DO WE BELIEVE IN SEVEN YEARS OF THE TRIBULATION PERIOD?

To understand the seven years of the Tribulation Period, we have to understand the meaning of Daniel 9:24-27:

> *Daniel 9:24-27:* Seventy weeks are decreed about your people and your holy city—to bring the rebellion to an end, to put a stop to sin, to wipe away injustice, to bring in everlasting righteousness, to seal up vision and prophecy, and to anoint the most holy place. Know and understand this: From the issuing of the decree to restore and rebuild Jerusalem until Messiah the Prince will be seven weeks and 62 weeks. It will be rebuilt with a plaza and a moat, but in difficult times. After those 62 weeks the Messiah will be cut off and will have nothing. The people of the coming prince will destroy the city and the sanctuary. The end will come with a flood, and until the end there will be war; desolations are decreed. He will make a firm covenant with many for one week, but in the middle of the week he will put a stop to sacrifice and offering. And the abomination of desolation will be on a wing of the temple until the decreed destruction is poured out on the desolator.

In the Jewish calendar a "week" means seven days, but it can also mean seven years. That is the case in Daniel 9:24-27. Daniel says in v. 24 that seventy weeks, or 490 years, was a time decreed to *"your people"* (Israel) and to *"your holy city"* (Jerusalem) to bring an end to sin. The seventy weeks begins when the command to rebuild the wall around Jerusalem is given. That command is given in Nehemiah 2:1-10. From the command in the 20th year of King Artaxerxes' reign to the entrance of the Messiah into Jerusalem as King is seven weeks (49 years) and 62 weeks (434 years), or a total of 483 years.

Sir Robert Anderson in his book, *The Coming Prince*, published in 1895, has been able to date the command to rebuild the wall of Jerusalem to March 14, 445 BC. Using the Jewish Biblical calendar year of 360 days, Anderson has calculated that seven weeks, or 49 years (445 BC to 396 BC), is the building of streets and walls in troublesome times (Nehemiah 2-6). Combining the seven weeks (49 years) with the 62 weeks (434 years) would equal 483 years.

483 years x 360 days (Jewish Biblical calendar) = 173,880 days.

Starting at March 14, 445 BC and counting forward 173,880 days, you get April 6, 32 AD. Anderson states this as the day Jesus rode into Jerusalem as the King of Kings (John 12:12-19).[16]

All that is left of the 70 weeks is one week, or seven years. This last week is the Tribulation Period, the time God promised to deal with Israel and bring an end to sin. Right now, God is dealing with mankind in a time period we call the "Church Age," giving everyone (Jews and Gentiles) an opportunity to be saved. But He has promised Israel one last chance to recognize and accept Jesus as Messiah. That last chance is the 70th week, the Tribulation Period.

In addition to Daniel's teaching of the seven years of Tribulation, the Book of Revelation reveals that the Tribulation Period will be seven years:

- Revelation 11:3 tells us the two witnesses prophesy for 1,260 days. Divide that by 360 days (Jewish Biblical calendar) = 42 months or 3.5 years.
- Revelation 12:14 tells us Israel fled into the wilderness for a time (1 year), times (2 years), and a half a time (half a year). Add those together and you get 3.5 years.
- Add 3.5 years of the two witnesses and 3.5 years of Israel in the wilderness and you get seven years of Tribulation.

The signs of the Tribulation Period are important, but not relevant if you have accepted Jesus as your personal Savior because you will be part of the New Testament church that is raptured before the Tribulation begins. Knowing this, what does God want you to do right now?

> *Matthew 24:42-44: Therefore be alert, since you don't know what day your Lord is coming. But know this: If the homeowner had known what time the thief was coming, he would have stayed alert and not let his house be broken into. This is why you also must be ready, because the Son of Man is coming at an hour you do not expect.*

If you are a believer, God wants you to be alert and ready because He could come for the church at any moment. But if you're not a believer, you can discover what billions of people have already discovered—Jesus saves! Give your life to Him today, right now, and you will receive eternal life and all the promises of Heaven! The Tribulation Period is described as the most terrible time in the history of the world. After reading this chapter, you can understand why Paul addressed Titus and described the Rapture as, *"the blessed hope"* (Titus 2:13).

7 POINTS OF REVIEW:

1. The primary purpose of the Tribulation Period is to prepare Israel for her Messiah. The secondary purpose is to judge all the unrighteousness and sin on the Earth.

2. Matthew 24:1-8 records three signs that lead up to the start of the Tribulation Period. They are religious deception (vv.4-5), wars and rumors of war (vv. 6-7a), and natural disasters (v. 7b). Matthew 24:9-14 records three signs that will happen during the Tribulation Period. Believers will be handed over to be persecuted (v. 9), defection of false believers from Christ (vv. 10-13), and declaration of the Good News to the world (v. 14).

3. There are 144,000 Jewish evangelists, 12,000 from each of the 12 tribes of Israel. They are called by God to be witnesses to the world. Their message is the message of the three angels found in Revelation 14:6-12. The first angel says to fear God, give Him glory, and worship the One who created everything. The second angel tells of the fall of Satan's kingdom. The third angel says to those who take the mark of the beast (666) they will be tormented day and night and there will be no rest for them.

4. The mark of the Tribulation Period is 666. The False Prophet administers it at the beginning of the Great Tribulation. It shows one's allegiance to the anti-Christ, and once taken it is irrevocable. The mark is

on the right hand or forehead, and is necessary to buy, sell, or trade. The mark will bring the wrath of God upon the person having it.

5. The two witnesses rise up at the beginning of the Tribulation Period. Their prophecy is for 1,260 days or 42 months or 3.5 years. They are killed and their bodies lie in the street for three and a half days. Afterwards they are resurrected and ascend to Heaven. Some believe the two witnesses could be Moses and Elijah because of the miracles performed. Others believe they could be Elijah and Enoch because neither died a physical death. Still others believe they will be two unknown believers that God will raise up at the beginning of the Tribulation Period.

6. There are 21 judgments of the Tribulation Period: seven Seal Judgments that are poured out on the Earth over years; seven Trumpet Judgments that are poured out on the Earth over months; seven Bowl Judgments that are poured out on the Earth over days. During these judgments, half of the Earth's population will die.

7. There will be people saved during the Tribulation Period. It is a salvation of endurance and faithfulness by refusing to take the mark of the beast (666).

5 BIG QUESTIONS:

1. What is the basic outline of the Book of Revelation as shown in this chapter?

_____

_____

_____

2. What are the three parts to the Tribulation Period? Describe them and list the events of each part.

_____

_____

_____

3. What is the Great Tribulation, and describe how it is different than the first half of the Tribulation Period?

_____

_____

_____

4. Who are the "The Four Horsemen of The Apocalypse?" What does each of the four horsemen represent?

_____

_____

_____

5. In your Bible, read Revelation 2:7, 11, 17, 29, 3:6, 13, 22. Now read Revelation 13:9. What is missing from 13:9 that is present in the other verses?

_____

_____

_____

Why do you think Revelation 13:9 is missing that last phrase?

_____

_____

_____

CHAPTER 6

THE SECOND COMING OF CHRIST

"The Tribulation Period is seven years, and when the signing of the covenant occurs, people who know the Bible and take it literally will know that, seven years later, Christ is going to come in His power and glory."[7]
Tim LaHaye, Author of *Left Behind*

There is something different about when guests arrive expectedly and when they arrive unexpectedly. Around 2008, I flew from Austin, Texas to Louisville, Kentucky to attend the Walker Family Reunion, my mother's side of the family. I didn't tell anyone I was coming, I just arrived. To see the look on my parent's faces when I snuck up behind them was priceless. My sister Dee blurted out, "Neale's here!" (reminding me of, "Ray's here!" from *Everybody Loves Raymond*). Mom whirled around with a look of shock on her face, and dad jumped up from his chair. They both had tears in their eyes, tears of joy. Needless to say, everyone was surprised to see me. All of my family came over to welcome me to the reunion and everyone gave me a hug. They were all glad to see me, and I was glad to see them. It was a great day.

When Jesus arrives on the Earth at His Second Coming, it will be the greatest day in the history of the world. There will be tears of joy in the eyes of those who have longed for His appearing. Romans 14:11 says, *"I live, says the Lord, every knee will bow to Me, and every tongue will give praise to God."*

Some would argue whether this is talking about the Rapture or the Second Coming. In my opinion, this has to be about the Second Coming because the Rapture happens so fast that only Christians are aware of what is happening. It's only at the Second Coming the entire world acknowledges Jesus as God and bows before Him.

So, we have arrived at the greatest event in the history of the world, the Second Coming of Jesus.

WHAT ARE THE SIGNS OF THE SECOND COMING OF JESUS?

Just as there are signs recorded in the Bible that usher in the Tribulation Period (Matthew 24:1-14), there are also signs that usher the return of Jesus (Matthew 24:29-44). The sixth and seventh Bowl Judgments begin the Second Coming of Christ (Revelation 16:12-21).

> *Matthew 24:29-31: Immediately after the tribulation of those days: The sun will be darkened, and the moon will not shed its light; the stars will fall from the sky, and the celestial powers will be shaken. Then the sign of the Son of Man will appear in the sky, and then all the peoples of the earth will mourn; and they will see the Son of Man coming on the clouds*

of heaven with power and great glory. He will
send out His angels with a loud trumpet, and
they will gather His elect from the four winds,
from one end of the sky to the other.

The first sign of the Second Coming will be total darkness on the Earth. You'll remember at the pouring out of the 6th Seal Judgment (Revelation 6:12-17), the sun turns black, the moon turns red, and the stars fall to the Earth. Then at the pouring out of the 4th Trumpet Judgment (Revelation 8:12-13), a third of the sun, moon, and stars are darkened. Now, according to Jesus Himself, the Earth will be thrown into total darkness—the sun will be darkened, the moon will not shed its light, the stars will fall from the sky, and the heavens will be shaken. I take that to mean there could possibly be some cosmic quake in the universe.

The second sign of the Second Coming is the appearance of Jesus, and all the people of the Earth will see Him coming. They will mourn because they will know instantly they have been completely wrong about Satan, the anti-Christ, and the False Prophet. That which they worshipped was not worthy of their worship. The unholy trinity was a fake and a fraud, and when the world sees Jesus they will realize just how wrong they were. It will be a day of mourning all over the Earth. Jesus will send out His angels to gather the elect from all over the world. Who are the elect? I believe they are the Jews and those who believe in Him during the Tribulation Period. Both did not take the mark of the beast (666).

The third sign of the Second Coming is in the Parable of the Fig Tree.

Matthew 24:32-35: Now learn this parable from the fig tree: As soon as its branch becomes tender and sprouts leaves, you know that summer is near. In the same way, when you see all these things, recognize that He is near—at the door! I assure you: This generation will certainly not pass away until all these things take place. Heaven and earth will pass away, but My words will never pass away.

This little parable reveals some important details about Jesus' return:

1. It is possible to know the general time of Jesus' return (v. 32). Just as a doctor can predict a general time a baby will be born, even though he can't determine the exact day an expectant mother will go into labor. When the Earth goes through these changes, it is like the labor pains before the baby is born.

2. You can know that Jesus' return is absolute (v. 33). Jesus promised He would die and be raised on the third day, and He did. Jesus promises He will return again, and He will.

3. Israel will play a key role in Jesus' return (v. 34). Look what the prophet Zechariah says:

Zechariah 13:8-9: In the whole land—the Lord's declaration—two-thirds will be cut off and die, but a third will be left in it. I will put this third through the fire; I will refine them as silver is refined and test them as gold is tested. They will call on My name, and I will answer them. I will say: They are My people, and they will say: The Lord is our God.

Two-thirds of the Jewish population will die during the Tribulation Period, but God will rescue a remnant of one-third. This generation of Jewish people will flee to Petra during the Tribulation Period. When Jesus returns, He will go to Petra and show Himself to the Jews, and the Bible says there will also be great mourning because the Jews will recognize that the Jesus they rejected over two thousand years ago was the true Messiah (Zechariah 12:10-12). Jesus will show them the scars on His hands, feet, and side where He was nailed to the cross for them (Zechariah 13:6).

4. The Parable of the Fig Tree reveals that Jesus' return is more absolute than the existence of the universe (v. 35). The present Heaven and Earth as we know it will die, but Jesus' words are eternal and will never die. Revelation 21:1 teaches, while the present Heaven and Earth will die, God will replace it with a New Heaven and a New Earth.

HOW WILL JESUS APPEAR AT THE SECOND COMING?

Revelation 19:11-16: Then I saw heaven opened, and there was a white horse! Its rider is called Faithful and True, and in righteousness He judges and makes war. His eyes were like a fiery flame, and on His head were many crowns. He had a name written that no one knows except Himself. He wore a robe stained with blood, and His name is called the Word of God. The armies that were in heaven followed Him on white horses, wearing pure white linen. From

His mouth came a sharp sword, so that with it He might strike the nations. He will shepherd them with an iron scepter. He will also trample the winepress of the fierce anger of God, the Almighty. And on His robe and on His thigh He has a name written: KING OF KINGS AND LORD OF LORDS.

Jesus will appear riding a white horse. Do not be confused with the rider of the white horse in Revelation 6:2, who is the anti-Christ. It is crystal clear this rider is Jesus because this rider is called Faithful and True. Jesus was faithful and true to do the will of God at His first coming by going to the cross (Luke 22:42). Jesus will also be faithful and true to the will of God at His Second Coming. Today, we need a standard of truth that is just and perfect. The reality is that truth is dying in America and around the world. We see corruption at the highest levels in Washington DC, on Wall Street, in the courtrooms, and in the boardrooms. But when Jesus comes, you will see perfect justice every time. Never again will an innocent person be falsely convicted of a crime they did not commit, nor will a guilty person be declared innocent for a crime they did commit. When Jesus comes, He comes as the Way, the Truth, and the Life (John 14:6), and He comes as omnipotent (all-powerful), omniscient (all-knowing), and omnipresent (all-reaching).

Jesus will appear as the Word of God (Revelation 19:13). Notice what John recorded about Jesus in John 1:

John 1:1, 14: *In the beginning was the Word, and the Word was with God, and the Word was God...The Word became flesh and took up residence among us. We observed His glory, the*

> glory as the One and Only Son from the Father,
> full of grace and truth.

Words have letters, and Jesus is the Alpha (first letter of the Greek alphabet) and the Omega (last letter of the Greek alphabet) as mentioned in Revelation 1:8, 21:6, and 22:13. Jesus is the beginning of everything and end of everything. Jesus was there at the beginning of creation, for John 1:3 says: *"All things were created through Him, and apart from Him not one thing was created that has been created."* And He will be there when the world as we know it comes to an end (Revelation 20:14-15).

Jesus will appear with armies (Revelation 19:14). Notice that "armies" is plural. I believe there are two armies that will return with Jesus. They are the army of the angels and the army of the saints. Why are the armies coming? The army of the angels is coming to assist Christ in the defeat of the anti-Christ, the False Prophet, and the worldwide army they assemble for the Battle of Armageddon at the end of the Tribulation Period. The army of the saints is coming to be revealed to the world as the bride of Christ (Romans 8:19), and to assist Christ during His millennial reign on the Earth.

Jesus will appear with a sharp sword coming from His mouth (Revelation 19:15). I believe this sword is literally the Bible, the Word of God. Ephesians 6:10-18 describes how a believer is to armor up for spiritual battles. Verse 17 says, *"Take the helmet of salvation and the sword of the spirit, which is the word of God."* Every piece of armor is defensive. The only offensive weapon we have is the sword of the Spirit—the word of God. Also, look at what Hebrews 4:12 says: *"For the word of God is living and effective and sharper than any two-edged sword, penetrating as far as to divide soul, spirit, joints, and marrow; it is a judge of the ideas and thoughts of the heart."* The sharp sword, which is the word of God, reaches to our very souls and judges every idea and thought we have. The word of God is everything to the Christian. When Satan strikes, the only weapon we have to retaliate is the Word of God. That's what Jesus used against Satan when He was tempted in the wilderness (Matthew 4:1-11), and that's what Jesus will use when He returns at the Second Coming.

Jesus will appear as "King of Kings and Lord of Lords." That's not the way He appeared the first time He came. The world did not recognize Him as King, and it still doesn't today. Many believe Jesus was a great teacher, a prophet, and wise man, but King of Kings and Lord of Lords? No! One of my favorite passages in the Bible is Isaiah 9:6-7. We read it often during the Christmas season because it prophesies about the coming Messiah. What I love about these two verses is how they describe two different periods of biblical history.

> *Isaiah 9:6:* For unto us a child is born, unto us a son is given. (KJV)

This has already happened. It happened over 2,000 years ago. No one really argues this fact because the whole purpose of Christmas is Christ. There are people that don't believe in Christ, but celebrate CHRISTmas.

The rest of this passage has not happened yet. This is referring to a future time that will take place at Jesus' Second Coming.

> *...and the government shall be on his shoulders. (KJV)*

This cannot be talking about Jesus' first coming because the government wasn't on His shoulders the first time He came. The government was the Roman Empire, who occupied Israel. But the government will be on His shoulders at His Second Coming because He will rule over the world for a thousand years.

And he shall be called Wonderful, Counsellor, The mighty God, The everlasting Father, The Prince of Peace. (KJV)

The first time Jesus came He was called "Rabbi," "Teacher," and "Prophet." It's only at Jesus' Second Coming that the world will recognize Him as "King of Kings and Lord of Lords."

Isaiah 9:7: *Of the increase of his government and peace there shall be no end, upon the throne of David, and upon his kingdom, to order it, and to establish it with judgment and with justice from henceforth even for ever. The zeal of the Lord of hosts will perform this. (KJV)*

We know at Jesus' Second Coming, that the kingdom He establishes is eternal. He will rule the world from Jerusalem sitting on King David's throne with David at His right hand. This kingdom will be perfect in justice and righteousness, and it will never end. It will last forever.

Isaiah 9:6-7, in my opinion, are two of the most powerful verses in the entire Bible. It declares what has already happened, and prophetically assures us what will happen, all culminating at the Second Coming of Jesus.

Jesus will appear to execute judgment on the ungodly of the Earth.

> **Jude 14-16:** *Enoch, who lived seven generations after Adam, knew about these men and said this about them: "See, the Lord is coming with millions of his holy ones. He will bring the people of the world before him in judgment, to receive just punishment and to prove the terrible things they have done in rebellion against God, revealing all they have said against him." These men are constant gripers, never satisfied, doing whatever evil they feel like; they are loudmouthed "show-offs," and when they show respect for others, it is only to get something from them in return. (TLB)*

When Jesus appears, He will return to the Mount of Olives east of Jerusalem, where He and His armies will immediately turn their attention to the anti-Christ and his army. Jesus will defeat them at the Battle of Armageddon using the sharp sword that comes from His mouth (Revelation 19:15), which is the Word of God. Not one shot will be fired. The total defeat of the enemy will be the words spoken by Jesus from the Word of God.

After the total annihilation of the enemy, Jesus will turn His attention to His chosen people, the Jews in Petra. He will go to them and show Himself to them and they will recognize and acknowledge Him as the long-awaited Messiah.

WHAT IS THE BATTLE OF ARMAGEDDON AND WHAT ARE THE RESULTS?

Satan will gather the largest army ever assembled from all the nations of the world. This army will gather in a place called Armageddon to go to war against Israel. But Jesus returns before the war can start.

> *Revelation 16:12-16: The sixth poured out his bowl on the great river Euphrates, and its water was dried up to prepare the way for the kings from the east. Then I saw three unclean spirits like frogs coming from the dragon's mouth, from the beast's mouth, and from the mouth of the false prophet. For they are spirits of demons performing signs, who travel to the kings of the whole world to assemble them for the battle of the great day of God, the Almighty. "Look, I am coming like a thief. Blessed is the one who is alert and remains clothed so that he may not go naked, and they see his shame." So they assembled them at the place called in Hebrew Armagedon.*

> *Revelation 19:19: Then I saw the beast, the kings of the earth, and their armies gathered together to wage war against the rider on the horse and against His army.*

Notice that when Jesus returns at the Second Coming, He returns with armies (Revelation 19:14), but when He goes to war against the Beast, the kings of the Earth, and their army, it's just Jesus and His army (Revelation 19:19).

This may simply be a grammatical device, but I believe it is possible that Jesus, and the army of the angels, will fight this battle, and the army of the saints will be spectators. Why do I believe this? For the same reason I believe Christians are spared the Tribulation Period: It is the wrath of God, and the saints are not meant for the wrath of God, but for the grace of God. So I believe it is possible we will see this great battle, but we will not be fighting in this battle.

There are three results of the Battle of Armageddon:

1. Blood will run 200 miles long, the length of a horse's bridle.

   Revelation 14:18-20: Yet another angel, who had authority over fire, came from the altar, and he called with a loud voice to the one who had the sharp sickle, "Use your sharp sickle and gather the clusters of grapes from earth's vineyard, because its grapes have ripened." So the angel swung his sickle toward earth and gathered the grapes from earth's vineyard, and he threw them into the great winepress of God's wrath. Then the press was trampled outside the city, and blood flowed out of the press up to the horses' bridles for about 180 miles.

2. All the dead bodies from Satan's army will become a feast for the birds.

   Revelation 19:17-18, 21: Then I saw an angel standing in the sun, and he cried out in a loud voice, saying to all the birds flying in mid-heaven, "Come, gather together for the great supper of God, so that you may eat the flesh of kings, the flesh of commanders, the flesh of mighty men, the flesh of horses and of their riders, and the flesh of everyone, both free and slave, small and great."...The rest were killed with the sword that came from the mouth of the rider on the horse, and all the birds were filled with their flesh.

3. The Beast and the False Prophet will be thrown into the Lake of Fire.

   Revelation 19:20: *But the beast was taken prisoner, and along with him the false prophet, who had performed signs on his authority, by which he deceived those who accepted the mark of the beast and those who worshiped his image. Both of them were thrown alive into the lake of fire that burns with sulfur.*

WHY DOES JESUS DELIVER THE JEWS FROM THE ANTI-CHRIST AT HIS SECOND COMING?

Jesus delivers the Jews because they are His people, and He promised they would always be His people. Israel is the only nation of the world that has a past, present, and a future. All other nations will cease to exist, but not Israel – it will last into eternity.

Jesus delivers the Jews because God promised Israel one last opportunity to recognize and acknowledge Jesus as their Messiah. Jesus' Second Coming is that last opportunity. While many Jews will choose to follow the anti-Christ during the Tribulation Period, a remnant of Jews will come out of the Tribulation Period seeing and believing Jesus as their Messiah.

Jesus delivers the Jews because the remnant of Jews from the Tribulation Period plays a key role in Christ's millennial kingdom. Biblical scholars have debated over the role of the Jewish nation during the millennial kingdom. Whatever it is, it must be an important one.

During the Tribulation Period, the Jews are persecuted more than any other time in history. When the persecution comes at the start of the Great Tribulation, the Jews will flee to Petra. This area today is south of Israel in the mountains of Jordan.

> **Revelation 12:6:** The woman fled into the wilderness, where she had a place prepared by God, to be fed there for 1,260 days.

When the anti-Christ moves his kingdom headquarters to Jerusalem, he puts a statue of himself in the Holy of Holies of the rebuilt temple and declares himself to be God. This is the Abomination of Desolation that is prophesied in Daniel and Matthew.

> **Daniel 9:27:** He will make a firm covenant with many for one week, but in the middle of the week he will put a stop to sacrifice and offering. And the abomination of desolation will be on a wing of the temple until the decreed destruction is poured out on the desolator.

> **Matthew 24:15-16:** "So when you see the abomination that causes desolation, spoken

of by the prophet Daniel, standing in the holy place" (let the reader understand), "then those in Judea must flee to the mountains!"

This is the trigger event that causes the Jews to flee Israel and Jerusalem for the mountains of Jordan to the area of Petra. Jesus delivers Israel from Satan in order to give them the land He promised them.

DOES THE BIBLE SHOW HOW THE WORLD WILL TRANSITION FROM THE TRIBULATION PERIOD TO THE SECOND COMING AND INTO THE MILLENNIAL KINGDOM?

Yes! Let's look at Daniel 12:11-12:

Daniel 12:11: *From the time the daily sacrifice is abolished and the abomination of desolation is set up, there will be 1,290 days.*

Daniel is referring to the Great Tribulation, which is 3.5 years (Daniel 7:25), or 1,260 days (Revelation 12:6). So what are the extra 30 days that Daniel mentions? I believe the extra 30 days are the Second Coming of Christ. It is during Jesus' Second Coming that He returns as "King of Kings and Lord of Lords" and judges the nations of the world. This judgment is called the "Nations Judgment" or the "Gentile Judgment." This is the second of three prophetic judgments recorded in the Bible. This judgment by Jesus is for those who accepted the mark of the beast (666). They are unbelievers and are defeated by Jesus and His armies at His Second Coming (Revelation 19:17-21).

Now look at Daniel 12:12:

***Daniel* 12:12:** *Blessed is the one who waits for and reaches 1,335 days.*

Following the Gentile Judgment, there is an additional 45-day period to set up Christ's millennial kingdom on the Earth. This kingdom is for those that did not take the mark of the beast (666), those who did not die during the Tribulation Period, and the saints (New Testament church and the Tribulation Period believers) who return with Jesus at His Second Coming.

So 1,260 days for the Great Tribulation; an extra 30 days (1,290) for the Second Coming to the defeat of the anti-Christ and his army, deliverance of Israel from Petra, and to judge the Gentiles; and finally, 45 days (1,335) to transition the world into Christ's millennial kingdom.

As we close this chapter, notice the contrast between Jesus' first coming and His Second Coming:

FIRST COMING	SECOND COMING
He came as a man.	He returns as God.
He came in peace.	He returns to conquer.
He wore a crown of thorns.	He returns wearing many crowns.
He came as the Word in Flesh.	He returns as the Word of God.
He came alone.	He returns with armies.
He came to serve.	He returns to be served.
He left under speculation about who He was.	He returns with no speculation about who He is.

7 POINTS OF REVIEW

1. When Jesus arrives on the Earth at His Second Coming, it will be a day of great joy because Jesus has kept His promise, and the long awaited prophecy of the Bible has been fulfilled. But it will also be a day of great mourning because those who made the choice to follow the anti-Christ and False Prophet and accept the mark of the Beast (666) will realize their eternal mistake.

2. Just as there are signs recorded in the Bible detailing the Tribulation Period, there are also signs in the Bible detailing the Second Coming of Jesus.

3. During the Tribulation Period, the Jews are persecuted more than any other time on Earth. The Holocaust won't look so horrible compared to the Tribulation Period. At the Second Coming, Jesus rescues the Jews from Petra or Edom and gives them the land God promised to Abraham in the Old Testament.

4. When Jesus appears at His Second Coming, He will appear riding a white horse with armies following behind Him. He will appear as the Word of God with a sharp double-edged sword coming from His mouth. He will appear as the "King of Kings and Lord of Lords."

5. At the Battle of Armageddon, Jesus will defeat Satan's army by throwing the army into a state of confusion. The confusion will come from the sword

that comes from Jesus' mouth. The sword is a metaphor for the Word of God.

6. The armies that come with Jesus at His Second Coming are the army of the angels and the army of the saints. The army of the angels will assist Jesus in the Battle of Armageddon and the defeat of Satan. The army of the saints will be spectators at the Battle of Armageddon but will assist Jesus during the millennial reign.

7. There is a marked contrast between Jesus' first coming and His Second Coming. In His first coming, He comes in peace, but in His Second Coming, He comes to conquer.

5 BIG QUESTIONS

1. In the Parable of the Fig Tree, Matthew reveals four important details about the Second Coming of Christ. What are the four details?

_____

_____

_____

2. What are the two time periods of Christ's coming that are described in Isaiah 9:6-7?

_____

_____

_____

3. What are the results of the Battle of Armageddon at Christ's Second Coming?

_____

_____

_____

4. Why does Jesus deliver the Jews? List three reasons:

_____

_____

_____

5. Give the meaning of 1,260 days, 1,290 days, and 1,335 days as mentioned in the chapter?

_____

_____

_____

CHAPTER 7

THE MILLENNIAL REIGN OF CHRIST ON THE EARTH

I continued watching in the night visions, and I saw One like a son of man coming with the clouds of heaven. He approached the Ancient of Days and was escorted before Him. He was given authority to rule, and glory, and a kingdom; so that those of every people, nation, and language should serve Him. His dominion is an everlasting dominion that will not pass away, and His kingdom is one that will not be destroyed.
Daniel 7:13-14

After the Rapture of the church, the seven-year Tribulation Period, and the Battle of Armageddon, Jesus establishes His kingdom on Earth. It will last 1,000 years. Why not just go straight to Heaven? I believe it's because Jesus needs to show humanity what a perfect world looks like. He needs to show the world that He is truly who the Bible says He is—"KING OF KINGS, and LORD OF LORDS," the One who is good, gracious, and glorious. He needs to fulfill prophecy from the Bible that shows Him ruling and reigning over the entire world (Isaiah 9:6-7). When He does this, there will be no excuses, and the world will not be able to say that they did not know who Jesus was or what He was like.

Dr. Billy Graham, in his book *Storm Warning*, says, "There can be no new world of lasting peace under present conditions. Something dramatic has to happen to alter human nature. That leaves us with only one absolute certainty about the future: Christ the Prince of Peace, with the government on His shoulders." Dr. Graham goes on to say; "Throughout the world today people crave a society of peace and provisions, but also one of goodness and justice. The Messiah Christ will implement all these, as 'with righteousness he will judge the needy, with justice he will give decisions for the poor of the earth,' as 'righteousness will be a belt and faithfulness the sash around his waist' (Isaiah 11:4-5) ... So transformed will the prevailing order be that even the animal world will be completely tamed: 'The wolf will live with the lamb, the leopard will lie down with the goat, the calf and lion and yearling together, and the little child will lead them. The cow will feed with the bear, their young will lie down together, and the lion will eat straw like the ox. The infant will play near the hole of the cobra, and the young child put his hand into the viper's nest. They will neither harm nor destroy' is the promise of the coming King (Isaiah 11:6-9)."[18]

WHAT'S THE PURPOSE OF THE MILLENNIAL KINGDOM?

It is to establish Christ as King over the entire world, to fulfill God's promises made to the world that cannot be fulfilled while Satan is loose on the Earth, and to instruct the inhabitants of the millennial kingdom in God's truth.

The millennial kingdom will look back, giving us a taste of what life would have been like had Adam and Eve not sinned in the Garden of Eden. But it will also look forward, giving us a taste of what life will be like in eternity in the New Heaven, on the New Earth, and in the New Jerusalem.

WHO WILL INHABIT THE MILLENNIAL KINGDOM?

The millennial kingdom will be inhabited by Jesus and six groups of people:

1. The raptured church.
2. The martyred saints of the Tribulation Period.
3. The remnant of Jews who did not follow the anti-Christ.
4. Those who survived the Tribulation Period by not taking the mark of the beast (666).
5. Those born that did not follow Satan at the end of the millennial kingdom.
6. The Old Testament believers.

WHAT'S THE MILLENNIAL KINGDOM GOING TO LOOK LIKE?

> *Isaiah 9:6b-7: ...and the government shall be upon his shoulder: and his name shall be called Wonderful, Counsellor, The mighty God, The everlasting Father, The Prince of Peace. Of the increase of his government and peace there shall be no end, upon the throne of David, and upon his kingdom, to order it, and to establish it with judgment and with justice*

from henceforth even for ever. The zeal of the Lord of hosts will perform this. (KJV)

Isaiah 11:1-9: *Then a shoot will grow from the stump of Jesse, and a branch from his roots will bear fruit. The Spirit of the Lord will rest on Him—a Spirit of wisdom and understanding, a Spirit of counsel and strength, a Spirit of knowledge and of the fear of the Lord. His delight will be in the fear of the Lord. He will not judge by what He sees with His eyes, He will not execute justice by what He hears with His ears, but He will judge the poor righteously and execute justice for the oppressed of the land. He will strike the land with discipline from His mouth, and He will kill the wicked with a command from His lips. Righteousness and faithfulness will be a belt around His waist. The wolf will live with the lamb, and the leopard will lie down with the goat. The calf, the young lion, and the fatling will be together, and a child will lead them. The cow and the bear will graze, their young ones will lie down together, and the lion will eat straw like an ox. An infant will play beside the cobra's pit, and a toddler will put his hand into a snake's den. No one will harm or destroy on My entire holy mountain, for the land will be as full of the knowledge of the Lord as the sea is filled with water.*

Revelation 20:4-6: *Then I saw thrones, and people seated on them who were given authority to judge. I also saw the souls of those* *who had been beheaded because of their testimony about Jesus and because of God's word, who had not worshiped the beast or his image, and who had not accepted the mark on their foreheads or their hands. They came to life and reigned with the Messiah for 1,000 years. The rest of the dead did not come to life until the 1,000 years were completed. This is the first resurrection. Blessed and holy is the one who shares in the first resurrection! The second death has no power over these, but they will be priests of God and the Messiah, and they will reign with Him for 1,000 years.*

WHAT WILL JESUS BE DOING IN THE KINGDOM?

Jesus will be ruling on the Earth from David's throne in Jerusalem (Isaiah 9:7). As Jesus is ruling over the world, I believe King David will be there with Jesus ruling over Israel.

Jeremiah 30:8-9: For it shall come to pass in that day, saith the Lord of hosts, that I will break his yoke from off thy neck, and will burst thy bonds, and strangers shall no more serve themselves of him: But they shall serve the Lord their God, and David their king, whom I will raise up unto them. (KJV)

During the millennial kingdom, there are at least three things Jesus will make certain to occur:

1. He will make sure the millennial kingdom is a time of peace.

Isaiah 2:4: *And he shall judge among the nations, and shall rebuke many people: and they shall beat their swords into plowshares, and their spears into pruninghooks: nation shall not lift up sword against nation, neither shall they learn war any more. (KJV)*

Could this mean that military equipment and military budgets will be used for agricultural means? Yes!

2. Jesus will make sure the millennial kingdom is a time of perfect justice. Today, we live in a society where justice is not dealt out fairly. But this will not be the case in the millennial kingdom. There will be perfect justice all the time and for everyone. Jesus, the perfect God, who is sovereign and knows all things, will rule in righteousness forever.

   Isaiah 9:7: *The dominion will be vast, and its prosperity will never end. He will reign on the throne of David and over his kingdom, to establish and sustain it with justice and righteousness from now on and forever.*

3. Jesus will make sure proper teaching of God's Word will be given to everyone.

   Micah 4:2: *"Come," they will say to one another, "let us visit the mountain of the Lord, and see the Temple of the God of Israel; he will tell us what to do, and we will do it." For in those days the whole world will be ruled by the Lord from*

Jerusalem! He will issue his laws and announce his decrees from there. (TLB)

How Will Jesus Teach the Truth of God's Word During the Kingdom?

No doubt He will use the latest and greatest technology including the Internet, social media, satellites, television, and radio. But Jeremiah 3:15 says that Jesus will also use shepherds who will lead the people in knowledge and understanding. I believe it's possible these shepherds could be the pastors, teachers, and professors we have today, those who have been given the spiritual gift of teaching by the Holy Spirit. Jesus will bring them to Jerusalem, instruct them in the truth of God's Word, and then send them out to the world. Jesus will use those already trained, but now with a complete knowledge of the Bible, to teach and instruct the people during the millennial kingdom.

Here's an incredible thought: Is it possible that God could use the actual people to teach about the actual events recorded in the Bible? Could it be possible that the apostle Peter will teach what it was like to step out of the boat in the raging storm on the Sea of Galilee (Matthew 14:22-33)? Is it possible the apostle Paul could teach about his experience of finding Jesus on the Damascus Road (Acts 9:1-9)? What about the apostle John? Is it possible that he could teach about what it was like to be called up to Heaven and told to write the Book of Revelation? Is it possible that Joseph could teach about what it was like to be locked away in prison for thirteen years only to rise as second-in-command in Egypt (Genesis 39-41)? What about Shadrach, Meshach, and Abed-Nego in the fiery furnace with the Lord (Daniel 3), or Daniel in the Lion's Den (Daniel 6)? Could Mary teach what it was like to be the earthly mother of Jesus? What about Noah, Moses, Solomon, Mary Magdalene, Lazarus, or the Gadarene Demoniac? Needless to say, the possibilities are endless, and we have 1,000 years to learn God's truth.

What Will the Saints Be Doing In the Kingdom?

First, and most importantly, we will be with the Lord. From the less than nanosecond we are raptured, we will be with the Lord forever. The apostle Paul reminds us of this fact:

> **1 Thessalonians 4:17:** Then we who are still alive will be caught up together with them in the clouds to meet the Lord in the air; and so we will always be with the Lord.

Second, we will reign with Him in new heavenly bodies free from sin, death, and sickness. Paul expressed to Timothy that one day we will reign with Christ.

> **2 Timothy 2:11-12:** This saying is trustworthy: For if we have died with Him, we will also live with Him; if we endure, we will also reign with Him...

In Revelation 20:6, John mentions five privileges of millennial believers:
1. We are blessed and holy.
2. We share in the first resurrection (the Rapture).
3. The second death has no power over us (first death is physical and the second death is spiritual).
4. We will be priests of God.

5. We will reign with Him for a thousand years.

Third, we will worship Jesus.

> *Zechariah 14:20-21:* On that day, the words HOLY
> TO THE LORD will be on the bells of the horses.
> The pots in the house of the Lord will be like the
> sprinkling basins before the altar. Every pot in
> Jerusalem and in Judah will be holy to the Lord
> of Hosts. Everyone who sacrifices will come and
> take some of the pots to cook in. And on that
> day there will no longer be a Canaanite in the
> house of the Lord of Hosts.

In the millennial kingdom, every aspect of life will be holy
to the Lord.

HOW WILL THE TRIBULATION SURVIVORS ENTER THE MILLENNIAL KINGDOM?

Those who survive the Tribulation Period and do not take
the mark of the beast (666) will enter the millennial kingdom
in their physical or natural bodies. How do we know this?

> *Matthew 25:31-34:* When the Son of Man comes
> in His glory, and all the angels with Him, then
> He will sit on the throne of His glory. All the
> nations will be gathered before Him, and He
> will separate them one from another, just as a
> shepherd separates the sheep from the goats.
> He will put the sheep on His right and the goats
> on the left. Then the King will say to those on
> His right, "Come, you who are blessed by My

Father, inherit the kingdom prepared for you
from the foundation of the world.

Those who Jesus separates to His right are called "sheep," and they will survive the Tribulation Period. They have not died, and therefore inherit the kingdom in their natural physical bodies. Because they are in their physical bodies, they will be able to procreate.

> **Isaiah 11:6-9:** *The wolf will live with the lamb, and the leopard will lie down with the goat. The calf, the young lion, and the fatling will be together, **and a child will lead them**. The cow and the bear will graze, their young ones will lie down together, and the lion will eat straw like an ox. **An infant will play beside the cobra's pit, and a toddler will put his hand into a snake's den.** No one will harm or destroy on My entire holy mountain, for the land will be as full of the knowledge of the Lord as the sea is filled with water.* (Emphasis added)

The words "child," "infant," and "toddler" indicate that children will be born during the millennial kingdom.

Some theologians believe that not only will babies be born but they will not experience death in the millennial kingdom. If Adam (930 years), Seth (912 years), Enosh (905 years), Noah (950 years), and Methuselah (969 years) all lived to be over 900 years old, should it surprise us when Christ establishes His millennial kingdom on the Earth that people will live to be 1,000 years old?

Since people are born in their natural bodies during the millennial kingdom, they are also born with the sin nature.

Satan will be gone, but the sin nature will still be present in their lives. The Bible clearly states the sin nature will not go unpunished:

> **Jeremiah 30:20:** *His children will be as in past days; his congregation will be established in My presence. I will punish all his oppressors.*

> **Isaiah 66:23-24:** *"All mankind will come to worship Me, from one New Moon to another, and from one Sabbath to another," says the Lord. "As they leave, they will see the dead bodies of the men who have rebelled against Me; for their maggots will never die, their fire will never go out, and they will be a horror to all mankind."*

Remember, the millennial kingdom is not eternal Heaven. In eternal Heaven, there will be no sin. But during the millennial kingdom, sin will be present and visible. Isaiah 66:24 seems to indicate there will be a death sentence to those that rebel against the Lord, but they will not experience death during the millennial kingdom.

WILL PEOPLE NEED TO WORK DURING THE MILLENNIAL KINGDOM?

Yes!

> **Isaiah 65:21-23:** *People will build houses and live in them; they will plant vineyards and eat their fruit. They will not build and others live in them; they will not plant and others eat. For*

My people's lives will be like the lifetime of a tree. My chosen ones will fully enjoy the work of their hands. They will not labor without success or bear children destined for disaster, for they will be a people blessed by the Lord along with their descendants.

Houses will be built, clothes will be needed, and farming will possibly be the major industry. There will definitely be a work force in the millennial kingdom. But it will not be the saints who entered the kingdom in a new heavenly body. The Bible says we will reign with Him, not for Him. This work force will be comprised of those in their physical bodies—those who survived the Tribulation Period and those born during the millennial kingdom. It's important to understand that those who work will want to work. They will have a job that fits their talents. They will work with a joyous attitude and they will rejoice at what they accomplish.

One of the characteristics of the millennial kingdom is that people will be prosperous. There will be no poverty or poor people during the millennial kingdom. There will be no one who will be hungry or homeless.

Ezekiel 36:29-30: I will save you from all your uncleanness. I will summon the grain and make it plentiful, and will not bring famine on you. I will also make the fruit of the trees and the produce of the field plentiful, so that you will no longer experience reproach among the nations on account of famine.

WHERE WILL SATAN BE DURING
THE MILLENNIAL KINGDOM?

During the millennial kingdom, Satan will be chained up in the Abyss (the Bottomless Pit).

> *Revelation 20:1-3:* *Then I saw an angel coming down from heaven with the key to the abyss and a great chain in his hand. He seized the dragon, that ancient serpent who is the Devil and Satan, and bound him for 1,000 years. He threw him into the abyss, closed it, and put a seal on it so that he would no longer deceive the nations until the 1,000 years were completed. After that, he must be released for a short time.*

Satan is chained up in the Abyss because he is a liar (John 8:44). Remember, the millennial kingdom is a time of proper and true instruction of God's Word. If Satan is loose during this time, he would be deceiving and distorting the truth of God's Word, as he does today. The millennial kingdom is a time of truth, and there is no truth in Satan. God locks Satan away to ensure that only truth will be given during the 1,000 years of the millennial kingdom. But this is not the end of Satan. The very end of Revelation 20:3 says that after the 1,000 years of the millennial kingdom are over, Satan *"must be released for a short time."* I will discuss the reasons why Satan is released in the next chapter – Satan's Last Stand.

WHAT WILL EARTH BE LIKE DURING THE MILLENNIAL KINGDOM?

During the Tribulation Period, present Earth suffers a great deal. From the fire thrown down from Heaven, to the possible nuclear war, to the worldwide earthquake, the Earth goes through a multitude of changes. But the truth is, the Earth has been going through changes since the fall of man.

> **Genesis 3:17-19:** *And He said to Adam, "Because you listened to your wife's voice and ate from the tree about which I commanded you, 'Do not eat from it': The ground is cursed because of you. You will eat from it by means of painful labor all the days of your life. It will produce thorns and thistles for you, and you will eat the plants of the field. You will eat bread by the sweat of your brow until you return to the ground, since you were taken from it. For you are dust, and you will return to dust."*

This was not the Earth that God created and gave to Adam and Eve. The Earth before the Fall was not cursed. It was perfect. It was not filled with thorns and thistles. Adam didn't have to work the ground; the ground simply produced food for Adam and Eve to eat. It's possible, and in my opinion, probable, that during the millennial kingdom, the Earth will be restored to its original creation, and the curse on the ground will be lifted.

There will be a multitude of changes; most notable will be animal life.

> *Isaiah 11:6-9:* *The wolf will live with the lamb, and the leopard will lie down with the goat. The calf, the young lion, and the fatling will be together, and a child will lead them. The cow and the bear will graze, their young ones will lie down together, and the lion will eat straw like an ox. An infant will play beside the cobra's pit, and a toddler will put his hand into a snake's den. No one will harm or destroy on My entire holy mountain, for the land will be as full of the knowledge of the Lord as the sea is filled with water.*

Some believe the animals of the millennial kingdom will become vegetarians as they were before Noah's flood. But not just the animals, many believe the people of the kingdom will be vegetarians, too. If you study life on Earth pre-flood and post-flood, it's possible to come to the conclusion that humans were vegetarians before the flood. It was only after the flood that God gave animals to man as food to eat (Genesis 9:3).

WHAT HAPPENS TO ISRAEL DURING THE MILLENNIAL KINGDOM?

Israel has always been God's chosen people. That will not change during the millennial kingdom. The Bible indicates the nation of Israel will be restored to its original relationship with God.

> *Isaiah 62:2-5:* *Nations will see your righteousness, and all kings your glory. You will be called by a new name that the Lord's mouth will announce.*

You will be a glorious crown in the Lord's hand, and a royal diadem in the palm of your God. You will no longer be called Deserted, and your land will not be called Desolate; instead, you will be called My Delight is in Her, and your land Married; for the Lord delights in you, and your land will be married. For as a young man marries a virgin, so your sons will marry you; and as a bridegroom rejoices over his bride, so your God will rejoice over you.

During the millennial kingdom, the Jews will be married to Christ just as we are married to Christ. There are many times in the Bible when Israel is referred to by God as an unfaithful wife. Some Bible scholars believe the book of Hosea is an illustration, or an allegory, of Israel's relationship with God. Hosea (God) marries Gomer (Israel) only to see his wife run back to her former way of life. Over and over, again and again, the Bible shows how Israel runs from God only to see God bring Israel back to Himself. Isaiah 62:5 says, that God rejoices over Israel as a bridegroom rejoices over his bride.

During the millennial kingdom, the Jews will be lifted up to a higher position above the Gentiles. There are two categories of people who survive the Tribulation Period. There are those who took the mark of the beast (666). They were thrown into the Lake of Fire. Then there are those who did not take the mark of the beast (666). They were promised entrance into the millennial kingdom in their natural, physical bodies.

Now, those who enter the millennial kingdom can be sub-divided into two more categories. There are the Jews, who after the battle of Armageddon will be gathered up by Jesus from Petra where they had fled during the second half of the Tribulation Period. He will give them the land God promised Abraham in Genesis 15. Then there are the Gentiles. They are probably the work force in the millennial kingdom and may provide services for the surviving Jews.

> *Isaiah 49:22-23: Look, I will lift up My hand to the nations, and raise My banner to the peoples. They will bring your sons in their arms, and your daughters will be carried on their shoulders. Kings will be your foster fathers, and their queens your nursing mothers. They will bow down to you with their faces to the ground, and lick the dust at your feet. Then you will know that I am the Lord; those who put their hope in Me will not be put to shame.*

God will elevate Israel to a place where they will be famous and praised.

> *Zephaniah 3:20: At that time I will bring you back, yes, at the time I will gather you. I will make you famous and praiseworthy among all the peoples of the earth, when I restore your fortunes before your eyes. Yahweh has spoken.*

7 POINTS OF REVIEW

1. Dr. Billy Graham believed for there to be lasting peace in the new world, human nature must be dramatically altered. This altering will occur in the millennial kingdom when Jesus comes as the Prince of Peace and establishes a worldwide government with Himself as the King of Kings. This kingdom is so transforming that the animal world is tamed (Isaiah 11:6-9).

2. As Jesus leads the world from Jerusalem, He will make sure the millennial kingdom is a time of complete peace all over the world. He will make sure perfect justice is given to everyone, and He will make sure proper instruction of God's Word will be taught throughout the world.

3. As a way of properly teaching God's Word, it's possible that God could use the actual people to teach the actual events of the Bible. Moses could teach about the exodus of Egypt and the forty years in the wilderness. Daniel could teach about spending all night in the lion's den. Mary could teach about what it was like to be the earthly mother of Jesus. Lazarus could teach about what is was like to be dead four days and then resurrected by Jesus. John could teach about writing the Book of Revelation and as one can imagine, the possibilities are endless.

4. It is my belief, and also others, that there will be no death during the millennial kingdom. When

the curse of sin is removed, the longevity of life will once again be the norm. If Adam, Seth, Enosh, Noah, and Methuselah all lived over 900 years, then it is absolutely possible that those alive during the millennial kingdom will as well.

5. Satan will be chained up in the Abyss for the duration of the millennial kingdom. There can be no proper instruction in the truth of God's Word if Satan, the Liar, is loose to lead people astray.

6. During the millennial kingdom it's possible mankind and animals will once again become vegetarians, as many believe they were before the flood.

7. During the millennial kingdom, the nation of Israel will be restored to their original relationship with God (Isaiah 62:2-5). Israel is the only nation of the world that has a past, present, and eternal future. During the millennial kingdom, God elevates Israel to a position where they will be praised (Zephaniah 3:20), and He will give them the land He promised Abraham in Genesis 15.

5 BIG QUESTIONS

1. What is the purpose of the millennial kingdom?

    _____

    _____

    _____

2. What are the six groups of people that will inherit the millennial kingdom?

    _____

    _____

    _____

3. How will Jesus teach God's Word during the millennial kingdom?

    _____

    _____

    _____

4. What is King David's role in the millennial kingdom?

    _____

    _____

    _____

5. How do those who survive the Tribulation Period by not
    taking the mark of the beast (666) enter the millennial
    kingdom?

    _____

    _____

    _____

CHAPTER 8

SATAN'S LAST STAND

And when the thousand years are expired, Satan shall
be loosed out of his prison, And shall go out to deceive
the nations which are in the four quarters of the earth,
Gog and Magog, to gather them together to battle:
the number of whom is as the sand of the sea.
Revelation 20:7-8 (KJV)

As General George Custer approached the Little Bighorn River on June 26, 1876, he had a decision to make, attack immediately or wait until the next day. General Custer made the decision to attack. We now know, he made the wrong decision. He was severely outnumbered, which resulted in a sound defeat. No U.S. Cavalry soldier who fought beside him left the Battle of Little Bighorn alive. Custer's defeat came to be known as "Custer's Last Stand."[19]

At the close of the millennial kingdom, Satan is released from the Abyss for one last battle with God. But unlike Custer, I believe Satan knows he is a defeated foe. When he is released from his 1,000 years in prison, he will know his time is short as he enters his final act. He will be seeking to do as much damage as possible, and he will do everything he can to deceive as many kingdom kids (those born during the

millennial kingdom) as possible. Revelation 20:7-10 records
for us Satan's Last Stand:

> *When the 1,000 years are completed, Satan
> will be released from his prison and will go out
> to deceive the nations at the four corners of
> the earth, Gog and Magog, to gather them for
> battle. Their number is like the sand of the sea.
> They came up over the surface of the earth and
> surrounded the encampment of the saints, the
> beloved city. Then fire came down from heaven
> and consumed them. The Devil who deceived
> them was thrown into the lake of fire and sulfur
> where the beast and the false prophet are, and
> they will be tormented day and night forever
> and ever.*

WHAT ARE THE NAMES FOR SATAN RECORDED IN THE BIBLE?

1. Abaddon – Revelation 9:11
2. Accuser of our brothers – Revelation 12:10
3. Adversary – 1 Peter 5:8
4. Ancient serpent – Revelation 12:9, 20:2
5. Angel of light – 2 Corinthians 11:14
6. Angel of the bottomless pit – Revelation 9:11
7. Antichrist – 1 John 2:18, 22, 4:3; 2 John 7
8. Apollyon – Revelation 9:11
9. Beast – Revelation 17:8
10. Beelzebub – Matthew 12:24; Mark 3:22; Luke 11:15
11. Belial – 2 Corinthians 6:15
12. Devil – Matthew 4:1; Revelation 20:10

13. Destroyer of nations – Isaiah 14:12
14. Dragon – Revelation 12:7
15. Enemy – Matthew 13:39
16. Evil one – Matthew 13:19, 38; Ephesians 6:16
17. Evil spirit – 1 Samuel 16:14
18. God (with a small "g") of this world – 2 Corinthians 4:4
19. Great red dragon – Revelation 12:3
20. Guardian Cherub – Ezekiel 28:14, 16
21. Lawless one – 2 Thessalonians 2:8
22. Liar – John 8:44
23. Leviathan – Isaiah 27:1
24. Lucifer – Isaiah 14:12
25. Lying spirit – 1 Kings 22:22
26. Man of lawlessness – 2 Thessalonians 2:3
27. Morning star – Isaiah 14:12
28. Mother of Prostitutes – Revelation 17:5
29. Murderer – John 8:44
30. Object of horror – Ezekiel 28:19
31. Power of darkness – Colossians 1:13
32. Power of death – Hebrews 2:14
33. Prince of this world – John 12:31, 14:30, 16:11
34. Prince of the power of the air – Ephesians 2:2
35. Roaring lion – 1 Peter 5:8
36. Ruler of darkness of this world – Ephesians 6:12
37. Ruler of the demons – Matthew 12:24
38. Ruler of this world – John 12:31
39. Satan – Job 1:6; Acts 5:3; Romans 16:20; Revelation 20:7
40. Scarlet beast – Revelation 17:3
41. Serpent – Genesis 3:4
42. Son of Perdition – 2 Thessalonians 2:3
43. Tempter – Matthew 4:3

44. Thief – John 10:10
45. Unclean spirit – Matthew 12:43

As you can tell from this list, the Devil has various traits and personalities, but an important truth to remember is that he is the nemesis of everything. His ultimate purpose is to bring fear into your life and drive you away from God. He is present in many religions, but he is best known for his work in Christianity. His first appearance in the Bible is in the book of Genesis, where he convinced Adam and Eve to eat the forbidden fruit from the tree of the knowledge of good and evil in the Garden of Eden. His last appearance in the Bible is in the book of Revelation, where he is crushed and thrown into the Lake of Fire.

Satan is often described as a horrible creature with horns, a tail, and a pitchfork, but nothing could be further from the truth. In fact, Ezekiel 28:12-19 depicts Satan as just the opposite: *"You were the seal of perfection, full of wisdom and perfect in beauty...Every kind of precious stone covered you...You were an anointed cherub...From the day you were created you were blameless in your ways."*

Jesus calls Satan "the ruler of this world" (John 12:31). The Apostle Paul calls him "the god of this age" (2 Corinthians 4:4). It's important that you know he is not your friend; he's your Adversary, Enemy, and Tempter. He's a Beast, Destroyer, and a Liar. He's the Man of lawlessness, a Murderer, and a Thief. He's someone you need to stay away from, because he wants to kill, steal, and destroy everything about you.

WHAT INFORMATION DOES THE
BIBLE GIVE US ABOUT SATAN?

In a nutshell, let me give you twelve facts about Satan from the Bible:

1. Satan started out as an archangel or cherub. Lucifer was a protector of God's throne (Ezekiel 28:11-19). In Hebrew, Lucifer means "morning star" or "bright star."

2. Satan was cast out of Heaven because he became prideful and sought to raise his throne above God's throne (Isaiah 14:12-14).

3. Satan is beautiful (Ezekiel 28:12-13, 17). If Satan were ugly with horns and a pitchfork, no one would be drawn to him.

4. Satan is powerful (Isaiah 14:12-14 and Ezekiel 28:11-19). While these passages are addressed to the King of Babylon and the King of Tyre, it is the evil power behind the two kings that makes them applicable to Satan. Lucifer, or Satan, is the leader of an evil world system, and although it is invisible, it is very real. The power behind the kings and rulers of Tyre, Babylon, Persia, Greece, and Rome from the Bible, and other evil dictators that we have seen come and go throughout the history of the world, is none other than the one who got it all started, Satan, himself.

5. Isaiah 14:12-14 and Ezekiel 28:11-19, are what Bible scholars call "double-reference" passages. They have a direct reference to the context of the passage (the kings of Babylon and Tyre) and a second reference to a Biblical teaching, event, or person. This second

reference could be a past event, as is the case here with Lucifer's fall from Heaven. Or this could be a future event, as in the case of Daniel's Abomination of Desolation (Daniel 9:27). In 167 B.C., a ruler by the name Antiochus Epiphanies set up an altar to Zeus in the Jewish temple in Jerusalem and sacrificed a pig on the altar. This event is known as the "Abomination of Desolation." In Matthew 24:15, Jesus references Daniel's event with a second Abomination of Desolation that must be a future prophetic event. Most Bible scholars believe Jesus is referring to the anti-Christ when he puts a statue of himself in the temple built in Jerusalem during the Tribulation Period for the people of the world to worship (see Matthew 24:15-21; 2 Thessalonians 2:3-4; Revelation 13:11-15). Isaiah, Ezekiel, Daniel, and Matthew are all passages that give us a picture of Satan and who he will be at his last and final stand against God.

6. Satan is a murderer and a liar (John 8:44). He cannot speak the truth, ever. Every word that comes from his mouth is a lie. He was a liar from the beginning, and he will be a liar to the very end.

7. Charles Stanley, in his book *When The Enemy Strikes*, says that Satan uses four snares when he attacks you: debate, division, doubt, and deception. Dr. Stanley gives two examples from the Bible: Adam and Eve in the Garden of Eden (Genesis 3:1-13) and Jesus at His temptation in the wilderness (Luke 4:1-11).[20]

8. Satan is crafty, using fiery darts of temptation to attack you (Ephesians 6:11-12, 1 Peter 5:8). His objective is to draw you away from God; to distract you from doing God's will, to thwart God's plan and purpose

for your life, and to completely kill, steal, and destroy your life (John 10:10). He throws fiery darts at you to entice you to become a victim to sin. Ephesians 6:16 urges Christians to *"...take up the shield of faith, and with it you will be able to extinguish the flaming arrows of the evil one."* The fiery dart's battleground is the mind, and that's exactly what Satan used to get David to commit adultery with Bathsheba.

9. Satan cannot read your thoughts, and he cannot be everywhere at one time. Only God is omnipotent, omniscient, and omnipresent. Satan has had 6,000 years to become an expert at observational intelligence. He sees what you do, what you say, and how you act and react. Then he knows how and where to attack you.

10. Satan attacks you externally and internally. External attacks cannot be avoided 100 percent of the time. These attacks happen because we live in a fallen, sinful world. Internal attacks can be avoided 100 percent of the time. These attacks are about who's in control. In the Bible the book of Job tells the story of a man under external and internal spiritual attack from Satan. Job's external attacks are the death of his children, the loss of his possessions, and the painful boils on his body. His internal attacks are the emotional distress from the death of his children, the constant verbal abuse from his three friends, and the advice from his wife to curse God and die.

11. Satan lives on the Earth today (Job 1:6-7). He does not live in Hell. When God cast Satan out of Heaven, He threw him to the Earth (Ezekiel 28:17-19).

12. Satan only has as much power over you as you give him. God has given you the Armor of God as the means to defeat his schemes, trickery, and fiery darts (Ephesians 6:10-18).

MORE SPECIFICALLY, WHAT DOES THE BOOK OF REVELATION REVEAL ABOUT SATAN?

1. He has the anti-Christ and the False Prophet working for him during the Tribulation Period.
2. He appoints the anti-Christ as the rider of the first four Seal Judgments. If you're like me and interpret Revelation literally whenever possible, then these four riders must be actual riders. I believe all the riders are the same rider—the anti-Christ. He is given the task by Satan during the Tribulation Period to bring peace to the Earth, the white horse. As we have already discussed in chapter 5, the first 3.5 years of the Tribulation Period will be a time of peace on the Earth. The anti-Christ is going to be mistaken for the Messiah. During the second 3.5 years of the Tribulation Period the anti-Christ shows his true colors and brings war and bloodshed (red horse), famine (black horse), and death (pale green horse) to the Earth.
3. He is the angel of the Abyss. Satan rules the Abyss as his kingdom. Right now, it is located on the Earth. Notice in Revelation 9:2-6 that when the Abyss is opened during the Tribulation Period, smoke from the fiery furnace darkens the sun and sky on the Earth. Then locusts come out to sting those who do not have the seal of God on their foreheads. Finally,

those men of the Earth who are stung are tormented for five months. All this tells us that the Abyss, Satan's kingdom, is somewhere on the Earth, or more likely, in the Earth.

4. He kills the two witnesses of God who have prophesied for 42 months, or 1260 days, or 3.5 years (Revelation 11).

5. He is the fiery red dragon who tried to prevent Christ's birth (Revelation 12). The truth is Satan tried to prevent Christ's birth from the beginning. In the Old Testament, Satan tried on a number of occasions to annihilate the nation of Israel by sending foreign nations to defeat Israel and carry them off into exile. Each time God protected a remnant of Israel to keep the line of succession intact until Christ was born. After Christ's birth Satan tried to kill Jesus through Herod, who had all male babies two years old and under murdered (Matthew 2:16-18). If Herod had been successful, Jesus would never have died on the cross, been resurrected, and ascended to Heaven. As a result, Jesus could never return at His Second Coming, establish His eternal kingdom, and defeat Satan and throw him into the Lake of Fire permanently. In our modern day, many theologians believe Hitler's attempt to gas and kill the Jews during World War II was another attempt by Satan to annihilate Israel and prevent Christ's Second Coming and eternal kingdom on Earth.

6. He fights against the archangel Michael in Heaven. He is defeated and permanently thrown out of Heaven to the Earth. Enraged by his defeat, he turns

his attention to the woman, Israel, who had given birth to the male child, Jesus (Revelation 12).

7. He wages war and persecutes Israel during the Tribulation Period. This level of persecution is unlike anything Israel has seen in its history. When God protects Israel by providing a place in the desert for 3.5 years, Satan turns his attention and wages war against Israel's offspring, which I believe to be the Tribulation saints. Revelation 12 paints a very clear picture of Satan's hatred for God's Son, Jesus, and God's people, the Jews and Christians.

8. He is worshiped by the whole Earth. He speaks blasphemies against God, and is permitted to wage war against the Tribulation saints and conquer them (Revelation 13).

9. He raises up the False Prophet, who compels the Earth to worship the anti-Christ. The False Prophet is powerful and convinces the world to take the Mark of the Beast (666).

10. He is the scarlet beast of Revelation 17.

11. He is chained up in the Abyss during the 1,000 Year Reign of Christ on the Earth (Revelation 20:1-3).

12. He is released after the millennial kingdom for one final battle against God. He is defeated when fire comes down from Heaven. Satan is captured and thrown into the Lake of Fire, where the anti-Christ and False Prophet reside. The unholy trinity is permanently defeated and never heard from again (Revelation 20:7-10).

WHO IS THE ANTI-CHRIST, ALSO CALLED THE BEAST?

The Bible says a lot about this person who appears at the beginning of the Tribulation Period. Who he is and what he does is mentioned in the Old Testament books of Ezekiel 28:1-10; Daniel 7:7-8, 20-26; 8:23-25; 9:26-27; 11:36-45; and the New Testament books of 2 Thessalonians 2:3-10 and Revelation 13:1-10; 17:8-14. These passages reveal the following facts about the world ruler of the Tribulation Period:

1. He will not be revealed to the world until after the Tribulation Period begins (2 Thessalonians 2:2).
2. Right now, his identity is being concealed by the Restrainer, who is the Holy Spirit (2 Thessalonians 2:6-7).
3. He is a Gentile, who rises from the Roman Empire because his ancestry is of the people who destroy Jerusalem (Daniel 9:26).
4. He rises at the beginning of the Tribulation Period and has all the answers to all the world's problems. He will be known by his charisma and intelligence, but also by his craftiness and manipulation (Ezekiel 28:6; Daniel 8:25; Daniel 9:27; Revelation 13:1; 17:3).
5. He rules over the nations of the Earth by absolute power (Daniel 11:36) that he receives from Satan (Daniel 8:25; Revelation 13:2).
6. He signs a 7-year treaty with Israel, but breaks the treaty 3.5 years into the Tribulation Period (Daniel 9:27).
7. He introduces pagan worship during the Tribulation Period and sets himself up as god (Daniel 9:27; 11:36-37; 2 Thessalonians 2:4; Revelation 13:5).

8. He hates Israel and does everything in his power to destroy her (Daniel 7:21, 25; 8:24; Revelation 13:7).
9. He becomes the great adversary of Christ, the Prince of Peace (Daniel 8:25), of His ministry (2 Thessalonians 2:4; Revelation 17:14), and of His people, Israel (Daniel 7:21, 25; 8:24; Revelation 13:7).
10. Although he rules the world for the seven years of the Tribulation Period, his true evil and wicked nature is only revealed the last 3.5 years (Daniel 7:25; 9:27; 11:36; Revelation 13:5).
11. His worldwide rule will be terminated by judgment from God, and He will be thrown into the Lake of Fire (Ezekiel 28:10; Revelation 19:19-20).
12. His defeat and judgment will take place at the Second Coming (Daniel 7:22; 2 Thessalonians 2:8), which will reveal Jesus as the true Messiah (Revelation 11:15). The world, which the anti-Christ ruled over, will transition to Jesus' reign and become the millennial kingdom of the saints (Daniel 7:27).

WHO IS THE FALSE PROPHET?

The anti-Christ's right-hand man is the False Prophet, also called "the second beast" in Revelation 13:11-18. Notice what this passage reveals about the third member of the unholy trinity:

1. Many theologians believe the False Prophet will be a Jew because he rises out the land of Palestine (v. 11).
2. He is the leader of the one world religion and carries out the duties of the false religion of the Tribulation Period (v. 11).

3. He is influenced by Satan, just as the anti-Christ is (v. 11).
4. He exercises authority on behalf of the first beast, the anti-Christ (v. 12).
5. He forces the world to worship the anti-Christ (v. 12).
6. He is able to perform miraculous signs, even causing fire to come down from the heavens (v. 13).
7. Because of his miraculous powers he is able to deceive the inhabitants of the Earth (v. 14).
8. He forces the world to set up an image of the anti-Christ, who was wounded by the sword, yet lived (v. 14).
9. He has the power to breathe life into the image of the anti-Christ and cause it to miraculously speak (v. 15).
10. He has the power to kill those who refuse to worship the image of the anti-Christ (v. 15).
11. He forces the inhabitants of the Earth to receive a mark on the right-hand or forehead (v. 16). This mark is the number of the Beast, which is 666 (v. 18).
12. He has the ability to control the world's commerce, and only those who have received this mark will be able to buy, sell, or trade (v. 17).

WHAT IS THE UNHOLY TRINITY?

Just as God is Father, Son, and Holy Spirit, Satan is a copy-cat and will create during the Tribulation Period the evil opposite of God for himself. The unholy trinity, also called the Satanic trinity, or trinity of Hell, is made up of Satan, also referred to as the Devil or the Dragon in Revelation 20:2, the anti-Christ, and the False Prophet (Revelation 16:13).

To compare and contrast the Holy Trinity with the unholy trinity: the position of God, the Father, is assumed by Satan; the position of Jesus, the Son, is assumed by the anti-Christ; and the position of the Holy Spirit is assumed by the False Prophet.

WHY IS SATAN CHAINED UP IN THE ABYSS?

As we saw in the previous chapter, Satan is chained up in the Abyss to be kept from deceiving people during the 1,000 Year Reign of Christ. 2 Corinthians 4:4 says that Satan is the god of this age, and he has blinded the minds of unbelievers to prevent them from seeing the light of Christ. Satan has worked hard to defeat the gospel message. However, the millennial kingdom is a time when God's righteousness is on display and God's Word is properly taught. It is also a time when God will challenge fallen mankind under the most ideal conditions to be holy, righteous, and pure in their lives. Satan, and his temptations, will be removed so that mankind can show that he is separated from Satan's influence. If Satan were loose in the world, he would be constantly tempting and debating people and planting doubts and deceptions in their minds for the purpose of creating a division between them and God. Satan must be removed so that during the millennial kingdom, this does not happen. Therefore, at Christ's Second Coming, Satan is captured, chained up, and banished to the Abyss for the entire millennial kingdom.

WHY IS SATAN RELEASED FROM THE ABYSS?

Revelation 20:3 predicts Satan will be released for a short period of time. The King James Bible says a "season," which I would interpret to be three months. Others would say longer, maybe even an extended age. The important thing to know is that it will be long enough to deceive thousands, maybe even millions of kingdom kids.

When Satan is released, He will know that his time is short, so he will hit the ground running. He will come out of his prison roaring like a lion (1 Peter 5:8), spreading his evil influence (v. 8), and assembling a vast army ready to go to war against the Jews (Revelation 20:8-9).

Many people ask, "Why would God release Satan after having him chained up and locked away for 1,000 years?" I believe there are seven reasons why God releases Satan at the end of the millennial kingdom.

First, Revelation 20:8 clearly states that Satan is released to deceive the nations and to assemble an army for war against God's people, the Jews living in Jerusalem. Satan has not given up on his ultimate goal—to be God and to destroy everything God loves. Since the beginning of time, Satan, or Lucifer, has been jealous of God. He believes he is superior to God. It was this pride that caused his ejection from Heaven, and it is this pride that will lead to his ultimate and permanent demise.

Second, Satan is released to show the total depravity of the human heart. God has challenged sinful mankind on many occasions down through history, and mankind has failed to choose good over evil repeatedly. Walter Scott says, "Alas! What is man? He has been tried and tested under every possible condition, in every possible way—under goodness, government, law, grace, and now under glory."[21] David Jeremiah says, "Apparently Satan is released at the end of the Millennium to reveal that even under the ideal conditions of the kingdom, human hearts do not change... The fact that Satan is loosed at the end of the thousand years, and some people will still follow him proves how depraved man can be."[22]

Third, Satan is released because the kingdom kids (those born during the millennial kingdom) must be presented the choice between good and evil, just as you and I have been. God gives every person a choice to follow Him or to reject Him. From the beginning of time to the end of time, every person must be presented both good and evil. During the millennial kingdom, these kingdom kids have only been presented good. Satan is released to present to them evil.

Fourth, God releases Satan from the Abyss because many of the kingdom kids' sin nature has not been forgiven. When Adam and Eve sinned in the Garden of Eden, humanity inherited from them a sin nature. The kingdom kids, born to those who entered the millennial kingdom in their natural human bodies, still have the sin nature present in them. Even a thousand years of peace will not change their sin nature. Remember, the millennial kingdom is not Heaven, and Jeremiah 30:20 reminds us there will still be people causing problems. Although there is no death, there is a death sentence. Satan is released from the Abyss so the kingdom kids can be presented the choice to accept or reject Jesus. Those kingdom kids that accept Jesus as their Savior, their sin nature is forgiven.

Fifth, Satan is released to reveal all the unsaved in the world. God will cast them to the Great White Throne Judgment. John calls this judgment the "second death" in Revelation 20:14. The "second death" is not for believers because they were resurrected at the Rapture. The "second death" is only for unbelievers. Their judgment will be at the Great White Throne. I deal with this in greater detail in the next chapter.

Sixth, Satan is released so that God can remove all the unsaved in the world before He merges the millennial kingdom with the eternal kingdom. There can be no unbelievers in the eternal kingdom because there is no sin in the eternal kingdom. God releases Satan to reveal the true hearts of those kingdom kids who become Satan's army.

Seventh, God releases Satan from the Abyss because the Abyss is not Satan's permanent, eternal home. Revelation 20:9-10 says that as Satan's army marches across the Earth and surrounds the city of Jerusalem, then fire will come down from Heaven and kill Satan and his army. They are then thrown into the Lake of Fire. God releases Satan so He can cast him to his final destination, the Lake of Fire, where the Beast and False Prophet have been thrown.

Many of the kingdom kids, who have been properly instructed about Jesus for hundreds, maybe even a thousand years, will make the unfortunate decision to follow Satan upon his release. That's how powerful and persuasive Satan is. You and I need to heed Peter's words in 1 Peter 5:8: *"Be sober! Be on the alert! Your adversary the Devil is prowling around like a roaring lion, looking for anyone he can devour."* Satan's ultimate goal is to steal, kill, and destroy your life, and take you to Hell with him. Don't let him win. Choose Jesus!

When I was 18 years old I gave my heart to Jesus, and I have never regretted that decision. I made that choice because I wanted no part of Satan and his evil ways. Satan is about death and destruction, but Jesus is about life and liberty. I know I made the right decision, and today I live the abundant life. What about you? By rejecting Jesus, you have accepted Satan. Satan wants to take you to his eternity in Hell. But God wants to take you to His eternity in Heaven. If you choose Jesus, He has promised you an eternity in a New Heaven on a New Earth living in the New Jerusalem. When you look at both choices completely, there is really only one choice—JESUS!

So, at the end of the millennial kingdom, where is God? Still in Heaven. Where is Jesus? Still ruling and reigning on the Earth from Jerusalem. Where is Satan? In the Lake of Fire being tormented day and night forever and ever, never to be seen or heard from again. Satan's last stand ends with his final and permanent defeat.

7 POINTS OF REVIEW

1. Satan started out as an archangel or guardian cherub of God. Then he became prideful, thinking He could raise his throne above God. God kicked him and one-third of the angels out of Heaven to the Earth. Satan lives on the Earth today.

2. Isaiah 14:12-14 and Ezekiel 28:11-19, while addressed to the King of Babylon and the King of Tyre, respectively, are applicable to Satan because he is the evil power behind their reigns. Satan is the leader of the evil world system. He is the power behind every evil king and kingdom mentioned in the Bible, as well as every evil dictator we have seen rise and fall throughout the history of the world.

3. Satan cannot read your thoughts. He is a created being. Only God is omniscient, omnipotent, and omnipresent. While Satan can't read your thoughts, he can see how you act and react. It is through 6,000 years of observational intelligence that he knows how and where to attack you.

4. Satan attacks you externally and internally. External attacks cannot be avoided 100 percent of the time because you live in a fallen sinful world. Internal attacks can be avoided 100 percent of the time because you have the Holy Spirit living in you.

5. During the Tribulation Period Satan creates the unholy trinity to help him rule the world. This Satanic

trinity is made up of Satan, the anti-Christ, and the False Prophet. They are the evil opposite of the Holy Trinity made up of the Father, the Son, and the Holy Spirit.

6. Every person from the beginning of time to the end of time must be given the choice to choose good (God) over evil (Satan). The kingdom kids, born during the millennial kingdom, do not have that choice until the end of the millennium. Accepting Jesus as Lord and Savior is essential to salvation and eternal life in Heaven with Him.

7. Upon his release from the Abyss, Satan is so powerful and persuasive that in a very short period of time he will convince many of the kingdom kids born during the millennial kingdom to follow him. They will make up the vast army that Satan assembles to go to war against God and the Jews living in Jerusalem. They are defeated by God with fire from Heaven and thrown into the Lake of Fire.

5 BIG QUESTIONS

1. How does John 8:44 characterize Satan?

_____

_____

_____

2. According to Charles Stanley's book *When The Enemy Strikes*, as referenced in the chapter, what are the four snares Satan uses when he attacks you?

_____

_____

_____

Read Genesis 3:1-13 and write down how Satan used each snare against Adam and Eve.

_____

_____

Then read Luke 4:1-11 and write down how Jesus overcame each snare to defeat Satan.

_____

_____

189

3. What is the unholy trinity?

_____

_____

_____

Explain each person's role in the Tribulation Period.

_____

_____

4. Why was Satan chained up in the Abyss?

_____

_____

_____

5. Why is Satan released from the Abyss?

_____

_____

_____

CHAPTER 9

THE GREAT WHITE THRONE JUDGMENT

As I kept watching, thrones were set in place, and the Ancient of Days took His seat. His clothing was white like snow, and the hair of His head like whitest wool. His throne was flaming fire; its wheels were blazing fire. A river of fire was flowing, coming out from His presence. Thousands upon thousands served Him; ten thousand times ten thousand stood before Him. The court was convened, and the books were opened.
Daniel 7:9-10

Walk into any courtroom in America and the first thing you'll see is the judge's bench. It will be raised to give the appearance of authority. The person sitting behind the bench will be the judge dressed in a black robe. He is the final authority of everything that takes place in that courtroom. He will oversee the trial, listen to the evidence, and when the verdict is in, he will hand down his judgment. That's a large part of the justice system in America. The problem is, it's not perfect. There have been thousands upon thousands of people who have been wrongly convicted of a crime they did not commit. Imperfect justice has been a problem since the beginning of time. But there is one final judgment recorded at the end of time that will right every wrong. It's called The Great White Throne Judgment.

> **Revelation 20:11-15:** *Then I saw a great white throne and One seated on it. Earth and heaven fled from His presence, and no place was found for them. I also saw the dead, the great and the small, standing before the throne, and books were opened. Another book was opened, which is the book of life, and the dead were judged according to their works by what was written in the books. Then the sea gave up its dead, and Death and Hades gave up their dead; all were judged according to their works. Death and Hades were thrown into the lake of fire. This is the second death, the lake of fire. And anyone not found written in the book of life was thrown into the lake of fire.*

What Is the Great White Throne Judgment?

It's the final judgment. It's the judgment of the dead. It's the judgment of those who rejected Jesus as the Messiah. It's the judgment of the unsaved. While this judgment will be primarily concerned with judging unbelievers, there will be believers judged here. The kingdom kids who did not side with Satan after his release from the Abyss must be judged, and since this is the last judgment, they must be judged here. This judgment will come after the 1,000 Year Reign of Christ and before believers enter into the New Heaven and New Earth.

Some believe there is just one judgment. They believe The Great White Throne Judgment will be a time when all believers and unbelievers will be judged. Those whose names are found in the Book of Life will be judged and rewarded, and given eternal life. They are the sheep of Matthew 25:31-46. Those whose names are not found in the Book of Life will be judged, punished, and thrown into the Lake of fire. They are the goats of Matthew 25:31-46.

Whether you believe in one judgment or three judgments, what matters most is that you realize that every person will stand before Jesus and face judgment for the things done and not done in this life.

> *Hebrews 9:27: And as it is appointed unto men once to die, but after this the judgment.* (KJV)

I believe, and others with me that every person ever born will be at The Great White Throne Judgment, but not every person will be judged. Christians have been judged at The Judgment Seat of Christ, and unbelievers of the Tribulation Period at the Gentile Judgment. The only ones left to be judged are the Old Testament believers, all unbelievers, and the kingdom kids who were born during the millennial kingdom.

WHO IS THE JUDGE OF THE GREAT WHITE THRONE?

The Bible makes it crystal clear that Jesus is the judge of the throne:

> *John 5:22, 27: The Father, in fact, judges no one but has given all judgment to the Son...And He has granted Him the right to pass judgment, because He is the Son of Man.*

Acts 10:40-42: *God raised up this man on the third day and permitted Him to be seen, not by all the people, but by us, witnesses appointed beforehand by God, who ate and drank with Him after He rose from the dead. He commanded us to preach to the people, and to solemnly testify that He is the One appointed by God to be the Judge of the living and the dead.*

2 Timothy 4:1: Before God and Christ Jesus, who is going to judge the living and the dead, and by His appearing and His kingdom...

Judges in any judicial system try to be right, but sometimes they fail. A prime example is Joseph of the Old Testament (Genesis 39). Sold into slavery by his brothers, he was bought by Potiphar, an Egyptian officer and captain in Pharaoh's army. Potiphar put Joseph in charge of his household. Everything was working perfectly until Joseph became the object of desire for Potiphar's wife. Day after day she tried to seduce Joseph, but Joseph, being a righteous man, rejected his master's wife. Denied by this Hebrew slave, she falsely accused him, and Potiphar had Joseph immediately thrown in prison. Was Joseph guilty? No!

At the Great White Throne Judgment, Jesus, the Judge, will always be right, fair, and just. There will be no arguing. There will be no attorney. There will be no jury. There will only be Jesus. He has the right to judge because He is the perfect sinless One.

WHO WILL BE PRESENT AT THE
GREAT WHITE THRONE?

Three groups of people will be present at The Great White Throne Judgment. First will be the dead unbelievers. The journey to this judgment will come from every place imaginable (Revelation 20:13), and even the occupants of Death (the grave) and Hades (place of torment) will be released for this judgment. The Jewish concept of Hades is that it is a two-compartment place. One compartment is paradise. In the story of the rich man and Lazarus (Luke 16:19-31), Lazarus died and went to paradise by Abraham's side. The second compartment of Hades is torment. The rich man died and was buried. Then looking up into paradise, he saw Lazarus by Abraham's side and asked for Lazarus to come and cool his tongue with water, for he was in agony in this flame. Those on the torment side of Hades will be resurrected to The Great White Throne Judgment. These unbelievers will realize they condemned themselves by the choices they made. They will be judged and thrown into the Lake of Fire.

> **Revelation 21:8:** But the fearful, and unbelieving, and the abominable, and murderers, and whoremongers, and sorcerers, and idolaters, and all liars, shall have their part in the lake which burneth with fire and brimstone: which is the second death. (KJV)

I believe the second group of people at this judgment will be saved believers. That's right! If you are a Christian today, I believe you and I will be at this judgment, but we will not be judged. We have already been judged at The Judgment Seat of Christ in Heaven after we were raptured. Let me give you six reasons I believe we will be at this judgment:

1. Jesus will be at this judgment as Judge, and as His bride, we will be there with Him.

   1 Thessalonians 4:17: Then we who are still alive will be caught up together with them in the clouds to meet the Lord in the air; and so we will always be with the Lord.

   Once we enter into Jesus' presence, we will never leave it.

2. Revelation 3:9 says that those from the synagogue of Satan will worship at the feet of believers. The only time the unsaved could worship at the feet of the saved would be at The Great White Throne Judgment. Before this judgment, the unsaved are imprisoned in Hades. After this judgment, they are thrown into the Lake of Fire.

   Revelation 3:9: Take note! I will make those from the synagogue of Satan, who claim to be Jews and are not, but are lying—note this—I will make them come and bow down at your feet, and they will know that I have loved you.

3. During the millennial kingdom, believers in their new heavenly bodies are given authority to assist Jesus in judging the world. As Jesus is judging the dead at

The Great White Throne, I believe you and I will be there assisting Him.

1 Corinthians 6:2: *Or do you not know that the saints will judge the world?*

4. Revelation 20:12 and 15 indicate that the Lamb's Book of Life is present at this judgment. Recorded in the book are the names of the saints. I believe we, the saints, are present at this judgment as a witness to the names written in the Lamb's Book of Life. We are there to testify to the truth of God's Word.

    Revelation 20:12, 15: *I also saw the dead, the great and the small, standing before the throne, and books were opened. Another book was opened, which is the book of life, and the dead were judged according to their works by what was written in the books...And anyone not found written in the book of life was thrown into the lake of fire.*

5. If we are not at this judgment, where would we be? We can't be on the Earth because Revelation 20:11 says the Earth and Heaven have fled from the presence of Jesus. The dissolving of the present heavens is described in 2 Peter 3:10-13. The timing of this event will take place the day when God will judge the ungodly (3:7). So we can neither be on the present Earth or in the present heavens because they have been dissolved by fire (1 Peter 3:10, 13). We cannot be in the New Heaven and the New Earth because they are not ushered in until after The Great

White Throne Judgment has ended (Revelation 21:1). If the *"heavens"* dissolved is the universe as we know it, the only other place we can be present, is at this judgment that must take place in Heaven.

6. I believe we will see those we did witness to, but they did not get saved; those God told us to witness to, but we did not; and to those we had the opportunity to witness to, but we did not take the time. There will be great weeping on our part because we will realize that we should have done much, much, more.

The third group of people present at this judgment will be the kingdom kids, those born during the millennial kingdom that stayed true to Jesus and did not follow Satan. How do I know the kingdom kids will be judged here? It's the only place they can be judged. This is the last judgment before believers are ushered into eternity. Remember, Hebrews 9:27 says that every person will die and then face judgment. They have to be judged at The Great White Throne.

Standing before a judge in a courtroom may be intimidating, but that will pale in comparison to standing before Jesus, the righteous, sinless, and perfect "Kings of Kings and Lord of Lords." You might be able to conceal your crime before a human judge, but there will be no concealing a single thing you have done in your entire life, good or bad, before Jesus. He who is sovereign knows everything and is keeping track of everything you have ever done. How do I know? Because the Bible reveals there will be books at The Great White Throne Judgment.

WHAT ARE THE BOOKS AT THE
GREAT WHITE THRONE?

Revelation 20:12: I also saw the dead, the great and the small, standing before the throne, and books were opened. Another book was opened, which is the book of life, and the dead were judged according to their works by what was written in the books.

While I don't know how many books will be at the throne, there could be 10, 20, maybe even 100. Let me give you at least five books that I believe the Bible reveals will be at The Great White Throne Judgment:

1. The Book(s) of the Bible

John 12:48: The one who rejects Me and doesn't accept My sayings has this as his judge: the word I have spoken will judge him on the last day.

The Bible is the standard by which all mankind will be judged, whether saved or lost. God would not judge mankind without first giving them the Bible, God's instruction manual to salvation and eternal life. This is the sole reason you and I have the Bible today, to find salvation in Jesus and discover the way to eternal life.

2. The Book of Public Works

Matthew 16:27: For I, the Son of Mankind, shall come with my angels in the glory of my Father *and judge each person according to his deeds. (TLB)*

Revelation 20:12: *And I saw the dead, small and great, stand before God; and the books were opened: and another book was opened, which is the book of life: and the dead were judged out of those things which were written in the books, according to their works. (KJV)*

Dead unbelievers and the kingdom kids will be judged on their deeds. I take this to mean things done that are out in the open, things done publicly.

3. The Book of Secret Works

   Ecclesiastes 12:14: *For God shall bring every work into judgment, with every secret thing, whether it be good, or whether it be evil. (KJV)*

   Romans 2:16: *In the day when God shall judge the secrets of men by Jesus Christ according to my gospel. (KJV)*

   There is nothing hidden from God. He knows everything. God's eyes roam back and forth over the Earth. He knows every secret word and every secret deed. A criminal may be able to conceal his crime from the law, and he may even be able to conceal his crime from the judge and jury, but one day that crime will come to light when he stands before Jesus at The Great White Throne Judgment. The serial killer, who has buried the dead bodies of his secret deeds, will one day stand before Jesus, and all his secrets will be exposed by the Light of the World.

4. The Book of Words

Matthew 12:36-37: I tell you that on the day of judgment people will have to account for every careless word they speak. For by your words you will be acquitted, and by your words you will be condemned.

God knows every time His name has been taken in vain. He knows every time an unholy word has rolled off the tongue of man. He knows every time a Christian is verbally persecuted for their faith in Jesus by an unsaved person. He is keeping track of every word spoken by every person and recording it. The Book of Words will be opened and it will either acquit you or condemn you.

5. The Book of Life

Philippians 4:3: Yes, I also ask you, true partner, to help these women who have contended for the gospel at my side, along with Clement and the rest of my co-workers whose names are in the book of life.

Revelation 20:12: I saw the dead, great and small, standing before God; and The Books were opened, including the Book of Life. (TLB)

Revelation 21:27: Nothing profane will ever enter it: no one who does what is vile or false, but only those written in the Lamb's book of life.

The Book of Life means "book of the living." Why will this book be at the Great White Throne Judgment? For two reasons: First, the kingdom kids who did not follow Satan after his release and stayed true to Jesus may see their names appear in the Book of Life. Second, the Book of Life will be there as a testimony against unbelievers to reveal they did have an opportunity to believe.

The names in the Book of Life at the end of time are those saved believers in Jesus Christ. They will inherit eternal life in the New Heaven on the New Earth with a home in the New Jerusalem.

What Is The Judgment Of The Great White Throne?

Unbelievers are sentenced to eternal death, which is the second death. The first death is when the body separates from the soul and spirit. The Jewish belief is that the body goes to the grave, and the soul and spirit go to Hades. If one is saved, their soul and spirit go to the paradise side of Hades. If one is not saved, their soul and spirit go to the torment side of Hades. Lazarus went to the paradise side of Hades where Abraham was, and the rich man went to the torment side, where he was in torment (Luke 16:19-31).

The second death is when the soul and spirit permanently separate. Only unbelievers experience the second death.

Revelation 20:14-15: *Death and Hades were thrown into the lake of fire. This is the second death, the lake of fire. And anyone not found written in the book of life was thrown into the lake of fire.*

Revelation 21:8: *But the cowards, unbelievers, vile, murderers, sexually immoral, sorcerers, idolaters, and all liars—their share will be in the lake that burns with fire and sulfur, which is the second death.*

Believers do not experience the second death because their body, soul, and spirit are reunited at the Rapture.

Revelation 20:6: *Blessed and holy is the one who shares in the first resurrection! The second death has no power over these, but they will be priests of God and the Messiah, and they will reign with Him for 1,000 years.*

If there is a first death and a second death, then there must be a first resurrection and a second resurrection (John 5:29). The first resurrection is for believers, and it happens in three stages. The first stage is Jesus' resurrection on Sunday morning after being laid in the tomb on Friday. 1 Corinthians 15:20-28 states that Jesus' resurrection guarantees your resurrection. Verse 23 gives the order of the resurrection, and Jesus is the firstfruit.

1 Corinthians 15:23: *But each in his own order: Christ, the firstfruits; afterward, at His coming, the people of Christ.*

The second stage of the first resurrection is the Rapture. Notice in 1 Corinthians 15:23, that after Jesus' resurrection, at His coming, the people of Christ are resurrected.

> *1 **Thessalonians** 4:16-17:* For the Lord Himself will descend from heaven with a shout, with the archangel's voice, and with the trumpet of God, and the dead in Christ will rise first. Then we who are still alive will be caught up together with them in the clouds to meet the Lord in the air; and so we will always be with the Lord.

The third stage of the first resurrection is when the martyrs of the Tribulation Period are beheaded for not taking the mark of the beast (666). They are resurrected to Heaven and given a white robe.

> *Revelation 6:9-11:* When He opened the fifth seal, I saw under the altar the souls of those slaughtered because of God's word and the testimony they had. They cried out with a loud voice: "O Lord, holy and true, how long until You judge and avenge our blood from those who live on the earth?" So a white robe was given to each of them, and they were told to rest a little while longer until the number of their fellow slaves and their brothers, who were going to be killed just as they had been, would be completed.

The second resurrection is the resurrection of dead unbelievers to The Great White Throne Judgment.

Revelation 20:11-15: *Then I saw a great white throne and One seated on it. Earth and heaven fled from His presence, and no place was found for them. I also saw the dead, the great and the small, standing before the throne, and books were opened. Another book was opened, which is the book of life, and the dead were judged according to their works by what was written in the books.*

Then the sea gave up its dead, and Death and Hades gave up their dead; all were judged according to their works. Death and Hades were thrown into the lake of fire. This is the second death, the lake of fire. And anyone not found written in the book of life was thrown into the lake of fire.

The truth is that every person, whether a believer or an unbeliever, will have an eternity. The believer's eternity is in Heaven with God. The unbeliever's eternity is in Hell with Satan. Death has never been and never will be the ceasing of our existence. Even today, unbelievers are not completely separated from God. The spirit in their created body is what is stirred when Jesus saves them. If they are not saved before they physically die (the first death), then it is at the second death and second resurrection where they are completely separated from God and thrown into the Lake of Fire (Hell). This separation in the Lake of Fire will be the loneliness of all loneliness a person could ever experience. It will be complete and total darkness. Look what Jesus says in Matthew's gospel:

Matthew 8:12: But the sons of the kingdom will be thrown into the outer darkness. In that place there will be weeping and gnashing of teeth.

The sons of the kingdom are unbelieving Jews.

Matthew 25:30: And throw the useless servant out into outer darkness: there shall be weeping and gnashing of teeth. (TLB)

Reserved for the Lake of Fire is a flame that does not give off light. Every flame known to man gives off light, whether it is red, yellow, orange, white, or blue. But not so for the Lake of Fire. This flame will not give off light because Hell is total darkness. This permanent place of torment will not be on Earth because there will be a New Earth inhabited by believers for eternity. It will be somewhere outside in the universe, a place handpicked by God. It will be torment because it will be completely dark and lonely (Revelation 22:15).

I remember as a child spending the night over at a friend's house. His room was in the center of the basement. There were no outside windows bringing light into his bedroom. That night, when we went to bed and he turned out the light, it was pitch black. I couldn't see my hand in front of my face. I laid there in bed feeling scared and lonely. I doubt I slept all night. To me that's what Hell will be like, so dark that you can't even see your hand in front of your face. Needless to say, I never spent the night at my friend's house again.

What Does the Book of Revelation Reveal About Hell, the Lake of Fire, and Eternity For Unbelievers?

Today, we have reduced Hell to a laughing matter. It has become the subject of jokes, comic books, and cartoons. The world has taken Hell and put it on the same level as Heaven. Hell is just the other place people go to when they die. It's not so bad. The world has made it livable and removed the severity of it.

John reminds us in Revelation 20 that Hell is real. The rich man in Luke 16 found it to be a real place. He was tormented and in agony in the flame.

The Great White Throne reveals three facts about Hell (the Lake of Fire):

1. Hell is torment because of what is not there. In Hell there is no Jesus. He's in Heaven. The chorus of the great old hymn "When We All Get To Heaven" says,

> When we all get to heaven,
> What a day of rejoicing that will be!
> When we all see Jesus,
> We'll sing and shout the victory.[23]

There's no singing about Jesus in Hell, only cursing God (Revelation 16:11). There's no smiling face of Jesus in Hell. There's no presence of God to be enjoyed. There will be no love from Him ever felt.

In addition to Jesus not being in Hell, there will be no Godly mother or grandmother to love you unconditionally. There will be no Christian friend to bail you out of the mess you've made. There will be no relief from the torment and agony you experience (Revelation 14:11). And there will be no end, because it is the second death.

Growing up in Kentucky, the 5th grade class at my elementary school always took a field trip to Mammoth Cave National Park to tour the caves. The tour guides would lead us through the caves and explain the different formations and what each meant. They explained stalactites and stalagmites. At the very end of the tour, the guide would gather all of us in a big open space and tell us to stand still and don't move. Then they would turn out the lights. It was probably only for a few seconds, but for an 11-year old it seemed much longer. What I remember vividly to this day is the utter darkness. We were far enough inside the cave that no light could get through to us. People say that if left in total darkness for an extended period of time, one would lose their mind. It's said that in Dante's *Inferno*, there is a sign that hangs over the entrance saying, "Ye who enter here leave all hope behind." Where there is no Jesus, there is no hope.

2. Hell is torment because of what is there. God created Hell as a place for Satan and his fallen angels.

    Matthew 25:41: *Then He will also say to those on the left, "Depart from Me, you who are cursed, into the eternal fire prepared for the Devil and his angels!"*

In Hell is the worst company imaginable. Revelation 21:8 says the occupants of Hell are, *"the cowards, faithless, detestable, murderers, sexually immoral, sorcerers, idolaters, and all liars..."* In Hell, there will be life's memories. The rich man in Luke 16:27-28 remembered the lost condition of his five brothers.

Experts say that fire produces the worst physical pain known to man. John Wesley, the great Methodist preacher, said, "Put your finger in a candle. Can you bear it for one minute? How then will you bear Hell-fire? Surely it would be torment enough to have the flesh burned from only one finger; what then will it be to have your whole body plunged into the lake of fire, burning with brimstone?"[24]

3. Hell is torment because those who end up there will realize they could have easily avoided it. I believe part of the torment of Hell will be that the occupants will remember the gift of salvation they rejected. They will remember all the times that Jesus reached out to them in love, but they turned their back on Him. They will realize Jesus did not send them to Hell they sent themselves to Hell. The writer of Hebrews says 2:3, *"...how will we escape if we neglect such a great salvation?"*

Hell is real, and Satan wants to take as many people there as He can. But the good news is that God has given everyone a way out, and it's as easy as A-B-C. Admit that you are a sinner. Believe that Jesus is the Son of God and that He died for you on the cross. Then confess your sins and commit your life to Him. If you do, then John reveals in Revelation 21:1-7 what is awaiting you in eternity:

> *Then I saw a new heaven and a new earth, for the first heaven and the first earth had passed away, and the sea existed no longer. I also saw the Holy City, new Jerusalem, coming down*

out of heaven from God, prepared like a bride adorned for her husband. Then I heard a loud voice from the throne: Look! God's dwelling is with men, and He will live with them. They will be His people, and God Himself will be with them and be their God. He will wipe away every tear from their eyes. Death will exist no longer; grief, crying, and pain will exist no longer, because the previous things have passed away. Then the One seated on the throne said, "Look! I am making everything new." He also said, "Write, because these words are faithful and true." And He said to me, "It is done! I am the Alpha and the Omega, the Beginning and the End. I will give to the thirsty from the spring of living water as a gift. The victor will inherit these things, and I will be his God, and he will be My son."

7 POINTS OF REVIEW

1. The Great White Throne Judgment is the final judgment recorded in the Bible. It takes place after the 1,000 Year Reign of Christ and before believers are ushered into eternity in the New Heaven and the New Earth.

2. Jesus will be the Judge at this judgment. He is Judge because God has appointed Him. The Bible is crystal clear on this, and I know of no one that argues this fact. He is also Judge because He is the perfect sinless Son of God.

3. At the Great White Throne Judgment, there will be three groups of people: The first group will be dead unbelievers. According to Revelation 20:13, they will come from the sea, from Death (the grave), and from Hades (Jewish place of torment). The second group of people at this judgment will be Christian believers. They will be there because Jesus is there and they will be assisting Him. But they will also be there as a witness to the names written in the Book of Life. The third group of people at this judgment will be the kingdom kids who were born during the millennial kingdom. They have not been judged and this is the final judgment, so they must be judged here.

4. The judgment of The Great White Throne is eternal death, which is the second death. The first death is physical and happens when the body separates from the soul and spirit. The Jews believe the body goes

to the grave and the soul and spirit goes to Hades. Dead believers go to the paradise compartment of Hades, and dead unbelievers go to the torment compartment of Hades. The second death is spiritual, and happens when the soul and spirit separate for eternity. Only unbelievers experience the second death (see Revelation 20:6, 14).

5. Since there is a first death and second death, there must be a first resurrection and second resurrection. The first resurrection is for believers and happens in three stages. The first stage is Jesus' resurrection from the tomb on the first Easter Sunday morning (Matthew 28:1-10; Mark 16:1-8; Luke 24:1-12; John 20:1-18; 1 Corinthians 15:20-22). The second stage is the Rapture of the church (1 Thessalonians 4:13-18; 1 Corinthians 15:23). The third stage is the resurrection of those believers martyred for not taking the mark of the beast (666) during the Tribulation Period (Revelation 6:9-11). The second resurrection is for unbelievers and happens at The Great White Throne Judgment (Revelation 20:13).

6. Hell, the Lake of Fire is a real place. It's real because Jesus says it is real (44 times He mentions Hell in the gospels). The Bible reveals three facts about Hell. First, Hell is a place of eternal torment because of what is not there. There is no Jesus in Hell; He is in Heaven with His believers. Second, Hell is a place of eternal torment because of what is there. Hell was created for Satan, the anti-Christ, the False Prophet, and all dead unbelievers. Third, Hell is torment

because those who end up there will realize they didn't have to go there.

7. Satan knows he is a defeated foe of God and the evil archenemy of every believing Christian throughout history. Because of that, Satan's ultimate goal is to take as many people to Hell with him as he possibly can. Mankind is God's supreme creation, and Satan's one desire is to kill, steal, and destroy all mankind. Notice Satan doesn't attack the animal kingdom or nature like he does man. He uses predatory animals and the violence of nature only to kill and destroy man. Satan is no friend to man. He is a liar and the father of lies (John 8:44). But Jesus is the way, the truth, and the life (John 14:6).

5 BIG QUESTIONS

1. In Jesus' Parable of the Sheep and the Goats in Matthew 25:31-46, who are the Sheep and who are the Goats?

_____

_____

_____

2. Who will be judged at The Great White Throne?

_____

_____

_____

3. What is the Jewish belief about the two compartments of Hades?

_____

_____

_____

Who is released from Hades and judged at The Great White Throne?

_____

_____

4. Raptured Christians will be at The Great White Throne Judgment but they will not be judged. What are the six reasons given in the chapter to support this position?

_____

_____

_____

5. There may be more than five books at The Great White Throne Judgment, but what five books are mentioned? Give Scriptural references as proof.

_____

_____

_____

CHAPTER 10

ETERNITY IN HEAVEN

"It is no coincidence that the first two chapters of the Bible (Genesis 1-2) begin with the creation of the heavens and the earth, and the last two chapters (Revelation 21-22) begin with the re-creation of the new heavens and the new earth. All that is lost at the beginning will be restored at the end—and far more will be added besides."[25]
Randy Alcorn, *Heaven*

If you were to take a vacation to a place you had never been before, it would help if you knew everything possible about your destination. For help planning your dream vacation, you might contact a travel agency. They would tell you the best hotels, the best restaurants, and the best activities.

If you know Jesus as your Savior, Heaven isn't a vacation destination; it's your eternal destination. It's Jesus' hometown, and He is there right now preparing for your arrival (John 14:1-3). But the truth is, Christians know very little about where they will spend eternity.

I've sat through Bible classes for my undergraduate degree and studied in detail books of the Bible for my doctorate degree. In all those classes, the professors spent very little time talking about Heaven. Like most classes, the material at the end of the syllabus gets slighted because you get bogged down with the stuff in the middle. Revelation 21-22 is no exception. The most comprehensive teaching about the eternal destination of believers is the last two chapters of the Bible, yet many Christians have never taken the time to study them.

While I can't give you every detail about Heaven, let me highlight a few things that I hope will motivate you to find some additional resources to do further study. One that I would definitely recommend is Randy Alcorn's book *Heaven*.

What Is the Difference Between Creation In Genesis and Re-Creation In Revelation?

Take a look at the comparison below:

GENESIS	REVELATION
The Heaven and Earth are created (1:1)	The New Heaven and New Earth are created (21:1)
The night is established (1:5)	No more night (22:5)
The seas are created (1:10)	No more seas (21:1)
The sun is created (1:16)	No sun is needed (21:23)
The curse is announced (3:14-17)	No more curse (22:3)
Death comes to mankind (3:19)	No more death (21:4)
Sorrow and pain begin (3:17)	No more tears and pain (21:4)
Man is driven from the Garden of Eden (3:24)	Man is restored to Paradise (22:14)

WHAT DOES THE BIBLE TEACH
ABOUT PRESENT HEAVEN?

Present Heaven and Eternal Heaven are not the same place. Present Heaven is the place Christians go to when they die. It's temporary. Eternal Heaven is the New Heaven and the New Earth and the New Jerusalem. It's permanent.

The people that go to Heaven have one thing in common: they are sinners who have placed their faith in Jesus Christ. They have accepted Jesus' offer of forgiveness and they have repented of their sins. They have committed to living their life for Jesus, and the Bible teaches that when they die, they are transformed to Heaven (Luke 16:22; Luke 23:42-43; Revelation 6:9-11). As a pastor, I have presided over a number of funeral services for believers and for unbelievers. The one thing I always talk about is Heaven, the home for believers.

Present Heaven is a physical place with physical properties. Notice the actual physical details about Heaven from the following Scriptures in the Bible:

Jesus promised the thief he was going to paradise, a real place.

> *Luke 23:42-43: Then he said, "Jesus, remember me when You come into Your kingdom!" And He said to him, "I assure you: Today you will be with Me in paradise."*

Jesus is physically standing at the right hand of God.

> *Acts 7:55-56: But Stephen, filled by the Holy Spirit, gazed into heaven. He saw God's glory, with Jesus standing at the right hand of God, and he said, "Look! I see the heavens opened*

and the Son of Man standing at the right hand
of God!"

In Heaven people are standing before an actual throne and before the Lamb. They are wearing white robes and have palm branches in their hands.

> **Revelation 7:9:** *After this I looked, and there was a vast multitude from every nation, tribe, people, and language, which no one could number, standing before the throne and before the Lamb. They were robed in white with palm branches in their hands.*

In Heaven, there are living and breathing eagles flying and speaking.

> **Revelation 8:13:** *I looked, and I heard an eagle, flying in mid-heaven, saying in a loud voice, "Woe! Woe! Woe to those who live on the earth, because of the remaining trumpet blasts that the three angels are about to sound!"*

In Heaven, there are multiple armies riding white horses and wearing white robes.

> **Revelation 19:14:** *The armies that were in heaven followed Him on white horses, wearing pure white linen.*

Many people believe that Heaven is a figment of our imagination, or a state of being. They couldn't be more wrong. Heaven is a real physical place with real physical properties.

In recent years, people have claimed to have gone to Heaven. Don Piper believes he went to Heaven as his dead body lay in his car on an East Texas bridge. Glynis and I heard Don Piper speak in Round Rock, Texas. If we had any doubts (and we don't) that Heaven is a real physical place, Don removed those doubts. He spoke about the people he saw, about the doorway he walked through, and about the aroma he smelled. After spending 90 minutes in Heaven, there is no question in his mind that Heaven is a real physical place. The apostle John believes that Heaven is a real place. The entire book of Revelation is what John was shown when he was called up to Heaven. In Revelation 1:9-11, John was on the prison island of Patmos because of his faith in Jesus. He was in the Spirit and told by Jesus to write on a scroll what he sees and send it to the seven churches.

In present Heaven, believers will have a physical body. Enoch was taken to Heaven in his physical earthly body.

> **Genesis 5:24:** *Enoch walked with God, and he was not there, because God took him.*

> **Hebrews 11:5:** *By faith, Enoch was taken away so that he did not experience death, and he was not to be found because God took him away.*

Elijah was also taken to Heaven in his physical body in a chariot of fire.

> **2 Kings 2:11-12:** *As they continued walking and talking, a chariot of fire with horses of fire suddenly appeared and separated the two of*

them. Then Elijah went up into heaven in the whirlwind. As Elisha watched, he kept crying out, "My father, my father, the chariots and horsemen of Israel!" Then he never saw Elijah again.

In the story of Lazarus and the rich man, both men were depicted as having physical bodies. In Hades, the rich man had a tongue and a thirst and could feel pain. In Heaven, Lazarus had fingers, and if he had fingers, then I think we can conclude he had hands, arms, legs, and a torso—he had a body.

> **Luke 16:23-24:** *And being in torment in Hades, he looked up and saw Abraham a long way off, with Lazarus at his side. "Father Abraham!" he called out, "Have mercy on me and send Lazarus to dip the tip of his finger in water and cool my tongue, because I am in agony in this flame!"*

The martyrs of the Tribulation Period entered into Heaven and were given a white robe and told to rest. The white robe must be worn on a physical body. Nowhere in the Bible does it indicate that we are spirits floating around in Heaven wearing white robes.

> **Revelation 6:9-11:** *When He opened the fifth seal, I saw under the altar the souls of those slaughtered because of God's word and the testimony they had. They cried out with a loud voice: "O Lord, holy and true, how long until You judge and avenge our blood from those*

who live on the earth?"" So a white robe was given to each of them, and they were told to rest a little while longer until the number of their fellow slaves and their brothers, who were going to be killed just as they had been, would be completed.

Present Heaven is not your final destination. In Revelation 21:1, John said he saw a New Heaven and a New Earth, for the first Heaven and first Earth had passed away. I believe the first Heaven that passed away is present Heaven, the place where Christians go when they die.

What Is the Difference Between Present Heaven and Eternal Heaven?

While present Heaven is the place believers go when they die, it is not their eternal home. Present Heaven is separated from present Earth, but the eternal New Heaven will be on the New Earth.

Revelation 21:1-3: I saw a new heaven and a new earth, for the first heaven and the first earth had passed away, and the sea existed no longer. I also saw the Holy City, new Jerusalem, coming down out of heaven from God, prepared like a bride adorned for her husband. Then I heard a loud voice from the throne: Look! God's dwelling is with men, and He will live with them. They will be His people, and God Himself will be with them and be their God.

Important facts:

1. Present Heaven and present Earth will cease to exist.
2. The New Heaven and the New Earth are the same place.
3. In the New Heaven and on the New Earth, there will exist a Holy City called the New Jerusalem.
4. Heaven is always defined as the place where God dwells. Right now, God dwells in present Heaven. In eternity, God will dwell in the New Heaven, which is on the New Earth.
5. When man dwells in the New Heaven on the New Earth, God will dwell with Him. So, in eternity where man is, God will be also.
6. The reward of living a faithful life on present Earth is eternity in the New Heaven and New Earth where we will be God's people and God will be with us, and He will be our God.

Theologian and professor Anthony Hoekema, wrote in an article entitled "Heaven: Not Just An Eternal Day Off," "The New Jerusalem…does not remain in a 'heaven' far off in space, but it comes down to the renewed earth, there the redeemed will spend eternity in resurrection bodies. So heaven and earth now separated will merge: the new earth will also be heaven, since God will dwell there with his people. Glorified believers, in other words, will continue to be in heaven while they are inhabiting the new earth."[26]

So, in a nutshell, here's the difference between present Heaven and eternal Heaven: present Heaven is up there where God is, and eternal Heaven will be down here where God will be.

WHAT IS THE NEW HEAVEN?

As I have already stated, Heaven is always where God is. That's what makes it Heaven. The New Heaven is the new place where God lives. In the present Heaven, when believers die, they go to be with God (2 Corinthians 5:8). However, in the New Heaven, God will come to where man is and live with him. The Bible tells us that Jesus is preparing the New Heaven right now:

> **John 14:1-3:** *Your heart must not be troubled. Believe in God; believe also in Me. In My Father's house are many dwelling places; if not, I would have told you. I am going away to prepare a place for you. If I go away and prepare a place for you, I will come back and receive you to Myself, so that where I am you may be also.*

Use your imagination for a moment. I believe that Jesus created everything we see in the world (John 1:3), and He did it in six 24-hour days and rested on the seventh day (Genesis 1:1-2:3). So everything we see in the world—the mountains and the deserts, the oceans and the seas, the forests and the flowers, the sunrises and the sunsets, the wind and rain, the sleet and snow, even the cattle on a thousand hills were all created in six days, yet Jesus has been gone 2,000 years preparing our eternal home. How much more magnificent must the New Heaven and New Earth be than the present Heaven and Earth? It must be beyond our wildest imaginations! There is no way our finite minds can begin to comprehend the beauty of that place, even with John's description in Revelation 21.

I remember the first time I saw the ocean. I had gone to Florida with a couple of high school friends, and when we pulled out onto the beach and looked out at the water, it literally took my breath away. The first time I saw the mountains of Colorado was on a church ski trip.

As Glynis and I were riding up a ski lift, I looked across the horizon at the snow-capped mountains, I knew that there was a God, and He created all of this for my pleasure.

When you and I step into eternity in the New Heaven and New Earth, I believe there will be mountains and beaches and fields of flowers, even desert climates. I believe we will have most everything we have now, but it will be greater and purer. And to think that it was created for our pleasure for eternity. WOW! What an amazing God we have.

WHAT IS THE NEW EARTH?

Ecclesiastes 1:4: *A generation goes and a generation comes, but the earth remains forever.*

God created the Earth to last forever. The New Earth is a new version of the present Earth. This New Earth will be purified by fire.

2 Peter 3:6-7, 10, 12-13: *Through these the world of that time perished when it was flooded by water. But by the same word the present heavens and earth are held in store for fire, being kept until the day of judgment and destruction of ungodly men...But the Day of the Lord will come like a thief; on that day the heavens will pass away with a loud noise, the elements will burn and be dissolved, and the earth and the works on it will be disclosed...as you wait for and earnestly desire the coming of the day of God, because of which the heavens will be on fire and be dissolved, and the elements will melt with the heat. But based on His promise, we wait for new heavens and a new earth, where righteousness will dwell.*

I interpret this to mean that the present Earth must be purified by fire to rid it of all the sin, evil, wickedness, unrighteousness, and unholiness that has existed on the Earth since the fall of man (Genesis 3). The New Earth is a purified version of the present Earth. God won't start over with a new Earth any more than He started over with a new mankind after Adam and Eve sinned in the Garden of Eden. God continued with sinful man and began His plan to bring Jesus into the world to die on the cross for man's sins. There is a direct connection of the pre-Fall world with the post-Fall world. Likewise, there will be a direct connection between the old Earth and the New Earth. The New Earth will be like the Garden of Eden, only better.

There are three things the New Earth will not have that the present Earth does have:

1. The New Earth has no sea (Revelation 21:1). This does not mean the absence of large bodies of water. I believe there will be. However, I believe there will be a new arrangement of water on the New Earth. It's possible there is no sea in order to manage the increased population from the millennial kingdom. Remember, there was no death for 1,000 years, so the population of the Earth will increase dramatically. While there were most likely millions of kingdom kids

that followed Satan as he made his last stand against God, the vast majority of them did not.

2. The New Earth has no Hell. It is my opinion that Hell, the Lake of Fire, is in outer darkness somewhere in the universe.

   Matthew 25:30: And throw the useless servant out into outer darkness: there shall be weeping and gnashing of teeth. (TLB)

   The New Earth would not be the re-creation of the original Earth if the permanent, eternal place of punishment existed on it. There must be reserved somewhere in the universe a place for the Lake of Fire.

3. The New Earth has no sin (Revelation 21:27). Revelation 21-22 describes eternity in the New Heaven and New Earth, and nowhere does it ever mention sin. In fact, just the opposite is mentioned. In Revelation 21:4 John says, *"Death will no longer exist."* Death is a result of sin. If there is no death, then there is no sin.

WHAT IS THE NEW JERUSALEM?

1. It's a city. Fifteen times in Revelation 21-22, the New Jerusalem is called a city. The description of the architecture, walls, street, and foundation point out that the city is a literal place. A city is a place with buildings, streets, and homes. It has residents, visitors, activities, events, and gatherings. It has

music, arts, education, sports, and religion. I believe the New Jerusalem will have all these and more.

2. Our eternal home with Jesus is a place of no tears, no death, no grief, no crying, and no pain (Revelation 21:4). I believe when God wipes away the tears He will also wipe away every thought and memory that would bring those tears.

Isaiah 65:17: For I will create a new heaven and a new earth; the past events will not be remembered or come to mind.

Heaven would not be Heaven if you and I could remember the sinful things we did in our earthly body, or if we could remember someone we knew who is in Hell.

3. The New Jerusalem is a city with no night.

Revelation 21:25: Each day its gates will never close because it will never be night there.

This always brings up a series of questions: Will we sleep in Heaven? Will we need rest? In our heavenly homes will we have a bed? Honestly, I don't know. Since the New Jerusalem is an actual city, I do believe we will have jobs and work. I believe we will have to care for the city just like Adam and Eve cared for the Garden of Eden. We will work, so it is quite possible we will sleep and need rest just as we do now.

4. This city will be tremendous in size.

    Revelation 21:16: The city is laid out in a square; its length and width are the same. He measured the city with the rod at 12,000 stadia. Its length, width, and height are equal.

    Many people envision the city to be laid out in the shape of a cube that would measure 1,400 miles in height, length, and width. If the city were placed in the United States, it would roughly cover the Midwest part of the country. From the western edge of the Appalachian Mountains to the eastern edge of the Rocky Mountains, and from the Canadian border to the state line of Texas. If our home in the New Jerusalem is really an apartment or a suite and not a mansion (it's possible!), and we account for the buildings in the city to have 12-foot stories (10-foot stories is normal on Earth) there would be 616,000 stories in the city. How many people could live in this city? Millions, maybe even a billion. How would you like to have the suite on 616,000th floor of the Street of Gold Luxury Apartments? How would you like to exit the city through the northern gate and step into a winter wonderland and snow ski down a mountain, or exit the city through the southern gate and step into a tropical paradise and spend a long weekend at the beach with the bluest water you've ever seen? In the New Heaven and New Earth, it just may be possible.

5. The city has gates.

Revelation 21:12-13, 21: *The city had a massive high wall, with 12 gates. Twelve angels were at the gates; on the gates, names were inscribed, the names of the 12 tribes of the sons of Israel. There were three gates on the east, three gates on the north, three gates on the south, and three gates on the west...The 12 gates are 12 pearls; each individual gate was made of a single pearl.*

These gates are for beauty, not for protection, because these gates will always be opened, and never closed.

6. The walls of the city are 216 feet thick and made of transparent jasper.

Revelation 21:17-18: *Then he measured its wall, 144 cubits according to human measurement, which the angel used. The building material of its wall was jasper, and the city was pure gold like clear glass.*

In the Bible, walls were built for protection. In the eternal city, the walls are built for beauty.

7. The city has twelve foundations.

Revelations 21:19-20: *The foundations of the city wall were adorned with every kind of precious stone:*

the first foundation jasper (a reddish color),
the second sapphire (blue),
the third chalcedony (sky blue with streaks of other colors in it),
the fourth emerald (bright green),
the fifth sardonyx (a red stone with streaks of white),
the sixth carnelian (a fiery red stone),
the seventh chrysolite (yellow and gold color),
the eighth beryl (a sea green color),
the ninth topaz (a brownish gold stone),
the tenth chrysoprase (a blue-green stone),
the eleventh jacinth (a violet-purple stone),
the twelfth amethyst (a purple stone).

8. The main street of the city is pure gold.

Revelation 21:21: *The broad street of the city was pure gold, like transparent glass.*

This gold is transparent. Some Bible scholars believe the main street is the only street in the city. Since the city is built in the shape of a cube, 1,400 miles in height, length, and width, how can there be just one street? If this is true, then the street may resemble a spiral staircase possibly starting at the southern gates and extending to the eastern and western gates of the city and end at the northern gates. This is just a guess on my part.

9. The eternal city has no temple.

Revelation 21:22: *I did not see a sanctuary in it, because the Lord God the Almighty and the Lamb are its sanctuary.*

The temple, or sanctuary, represents a place of worship and a place to meet with God. This city has no need for a sanctuary because God Himself will inhabit the city. He will live in the city with us and make it His new home (Revelation 21:3).

10. The New Jerusalem is a city with a very bright Light.

Revelation 21:23: *The city does not need the sun or the moon to shine on it, because God's glory illuminates it, and its lamp is the Lamb.*

The light may refer to the Shekinah Glory of God. The light from Jesus will shine in all directions from the throne of God. This is probably why the material of the city is transparent. I believe there will be no shadows in the city, because a shadow is a form of darkness. But with the Lamb of the city as its lamp, there will never be light or darkness...ever!

11. There is nature in the city.

Revelation 22:1-5: *Then he showed me the river of living water, sparkling like crystal, flowing from the throne of God and of the Lamb down the middle of the broad street of the city. On both sides of the river was the tree of life bearing kinds of fruit, producing its fruit every month. The leaves of the tree are for healing the nations, and there will no longer be any curse. The throne of God and of the Lamb will be in the city, and His servants will serve Him. They will see His face, and His name will be on their foreheads. Night will no longer exist, and people will not need lamplight or sunlight, because the Lord God will give them light. And they will reign forever and ever.*

After the Great White Throne Judgment, the New Jerusalem will come down from Heaven (Revelation 21:2). Many scholars believe the city will descend to a point above the New Earth in the second Heaven, what we know as outer space, and will be suspended there for eternity. I have believed and taught the same thing, but I do not believe that to be the case now. I agree with Randy Alcorn, who teaches in his book *Heaven*, that the New Jerusalem will be on the New Earth. I also believe the throne of God, which could be at the center of the New Jerusalem, will be located at the current city of Jerusalem. The Bible says that Jesus will rule the millennial kingdom from David's throne in Jerusalem (Isaiah 9:7). It's possible, maybe even probable, that Jesus will continue to rule over the New Heaven and New Earth from God's throne in the New Jerusalem.

WHO ARE THE NATIONS AND THE KINGS OF THE EARTH IN REVELATION 21:24?

They are not sinners. Remember, the present Earth has passed away (21:1) and along with it sin, evil, wickedness, and unrighteousness. There is now a New Heaven and a New Earth, where the previous things have passed away (21:4). There are two lists of people in Revelation 21:8 and 22:15. These are sinners, and John is crystal clear that these are not anywhere on the New Earth. They are in the Lake of Fire.

So who are the nations and their kings? I believe they are part of the "victors" mentioned in 21:7. While they do not inherit the New Jerusalem, they have come to recognize

Jesus as Messiah. These are the multitude of nations that come out of the Tribulation Period, having not taken the mark of the beast (666), and they are also the kingdom kids who did not follow Satan at his last stand. They are made up from every ethnic nation on the present Earth. They are definitely believers because v. 27 says that nothing profane can enter the city, and no one who does what is vile or false, only those whose names are written in the Lamb's book of life. I believe Israel is absolutely included among these nations. The Bible clearly states that Israel not only has a past and present but it also has a forever future even in the New Heaven and Earth (see Isaiah 66:22, Zephaniah 3:20).

While these nations do not live in the New Jerusalem, they do have access to the holy city. They bring their glory and honor into the city to worship and praise Jesus. As they arrive to worship, the gates of the holy city are open to them. They come and go just like the inhabitants of the city. Every day in the eternal city is a day of righteousness, holiness, and purity.

7 POINTS OF REVIEW:

1. The Bible teaches that there is a difference between present Heaven, the place Christians go when they die, and eternal Heaven, the place Christians will live with God forever.

2. Heaven is always defined as where God is. Right now, God is up there in present Heaven. In eternity, the New Heaven will be down here where God will be (Revelation 21:1-3).

3. The New Earth is new in the sense that it is purified of all the sin, evil, wickedness, and unrighteousness. The New Earth will be like the Garden of Eden, only better.

4. The New Jerusalem is an actual city just as the New Heaven and New Earth are actual places. This new city will be in the New Heaven and the New Earth.

5. The New Jerusalem has no temple because it doesn't need one. A temple is a place to worship and meet with God. The New Jerusalem doesn't need a place to meet with God because God will live in the city with believers.

6. There are two settings of nature in the New Jerusalem as mentioned in Revelation 22:1-3. A river from the throne of God will flow down the middle of the city's main street, and the tree of life producing twelve different kinds of fruit each month. Many

scholars believe the residents of the New Earth will revert back to a possible pre-Flood vegetarian diet. The leaves of the tree of life will be used for healing the nations.

7. Revelation 21:24 says, *"The nations will walk in its light, and the kings of the earth will bring their glory into it."* The nations and the kings of the New Earth, who bring their glory into the New Jerusalem, are two groups of people. The first is those who come out of the Tribulation Period having not taken the mark of the beast (666). Included in this group are the Jews that fled to Petra and will be rescued by Jesus at His Second Coming. The second group will be the kingdom kids who do not follow Satan in his final rebellion against God. They come from every ethnic nation of the present Earth. It's important to remember they are saved believers, or they would not be present on the New Earth.

5 BIG QUESTIONS:

1. What is the difference between creation in Genesis 1-2 and re-creation in Revelation 21-22?

_____

_____

_____

2. What are four things about the present Heaven that show it is a real place not just a figment of our imagination?

_____

_____

_____

3. What are the three things the New Earth will have that present Earth does not have?

_____

_____

_____

4. What are the physical dimensions of the New Jerusalem?

_____

_____

_____

In your opinion, what is the purpose of jasper walls, the pearl gates, the gold street, and the twelve foundations of different stones?

_____

_____

_____

5. Taking in consideration the physical description from Revelation 21:9-27, try to express in words the beauty of the New Jerusalem, the holy city.

_____

_____

_____

BIBLIOGRAPHY

Alcorn, Randy. *Heaven*. Carol Stream, Ill: Tyndale, 2004.

Anderson, Sir Robert. *The Coming Prince*. Grand Rapids, MI: Kregel Classics, 1957.

Eareckson-Tada, Joni. *Heaven: Your Real Home*. Grand Rapids, MI: Zondervan, 1995.

Edwards, Randy. *Eschatology I*. Taped Lectures. Andersonville Baptist Seminary, Camilla, GA: 2000.

Graham, Billy. *Storm Warning*. Dallas, TX: Word Publishing, 1992.

Hanegraaf, Hank. *Resurrection*. Nashville, TN: Thomas Nelson, 2000.

Jeremiah, David. *Escape the Coming Night*. Nashville, TN: W Publishing, 2018.

Pentecost, J. Dwight. *Things To Come*. Grand Rapids, MI: Zondervan, 1958.

Scott, Walter. *Exposition of the Revelation of Jesus Christ*. London: Pickering and Inglis, n.d.

Stanley, Charles. *When The Enemy Strikes*. Nashville, TN: Nelson Books, 2004.

Warren, Rick. *The Purpose Driven Life*. Grand Rapids, MI: Zondervan, 2002.

GLOSSARY

A –

Abomination of Desolation – When the anti-Christ goes into the Tribulation temple and declares himself to be God. This is prophesied in Daniel 9:27, 12:11, Matthew 24:15, and 2 Thessalonians 2:4

Abyss – The place Satan is chained and locked away in during Jesus' 1,000 Year Reign on the Earth.

Age of Accountability – The belief that those who die before reaching the ability to make a choice to accept or reject Jesus are saved by God's grace and mercy.

Age of Grace – The time period when the followers of Jesus are saved by grace. It starts at Pentecost (Acts 2) and extends to the Rapture. Also called the Church Age.

Antichrist – The world ruler during the Tribulation Period. Part of the unholy trinity with Satan and the False Prophet.

B –

Battle of Armageddon – The battle between Christ and His army of angels and the anti-Christ and his worldwide army.

Christ defeats the anti-Christ and throws he and the False Prophet into the Lake of Fire.

Beast – Another name for the anti-Christ.

Bema Judgment – Another name for the Judgment Seat of Christ.

Book of Life – Contains the names of every believer who has acknowledged and accepted Jesus Christ as their Savior.

Bowl Judgments – The final set of 7 judgments of God on the Earth during the Tribulation Period. See Revelation 16. These judgments are poured out on the Earth over the course of days.

D –

Dispensationalism – The theological belief that recognized seven administrations to God's plan for humanity: Innocence (Genesis 1:1-3:17), Conscience (Genesis 3:8-8:22), Human government (Genesis 9:1-11:32), Promise (Genesis 12:1-Exodus 19:25), Law (Exodus 20:1-Acts 2:4), Grace (Acts 2:4-Revelation 20:3), and Millennial Kingdom (Revelation 20:4-6). Dispensationalism has three primary beliefs: 1). God will keep His promises to both Israel and the church. He has a separate plan for both, and the church has not replaced Israel as God's people or in God's plan. 2). The Bible should be read and interpreted in the most plain, ordinary, normal manner, and as literally as possible. Allowances are made for symbols, figurative language, and metaphors. But even these have a literal meaning behind them. 3). God does all things to reveal His glory to His creation.

Dispensationalist – Holds to a literal interpretation of the Bible and usually holds a pre-Tribulation view of the Rapture and a pre-millennial view of the Second Coming.

E –

Earthly body – Your natural body that you were born into. It is a body of flesh.

Edom – The place the Jews flee to when the anti-Christ moves his headquarters from Babylon to Jerusalem. Edom is located in the mountains of Jordan south of Israel. It is also called Petra.

Eternal life – The reward given to a person who accepts Jesus as their Savior in this life. While the physical body will die, the soul and spirit will live in eternity.

Eternity – Life in the New Heaven and New Earth. No one dies in eternity. Life is eternal and everlasting.

F –

False Prophet – The anti-Christ's right-hand man. He is the leader of a one-world religion during the Tribulation Period.

Flesh – Your earthly natural body in which you were born. The flesh is sinful, mortal, and weak.

First death – Physical death. When the soul and spirit separates from the body.

First resurrection – The resurrection for Christ and His followers. It happens in three stages. First, Christ's resurrection on the first Easter Sunday morning. Second, the Rapture of all Christian believers. Third, the martyrs killed during the Tribulation Period.

G –

Gentile Judgment – The second of three judgments. It takes place at Christ's second coming and is for those who took the mark of the beast (666). Also called the Nation's Judgment.

Gospel – God's message to the world that Jesus is the Messiah, and those who accept Him are promised eternal life in Heaven.

Great Commission – The command given to the church to go into the world and share the gospel, making disciples, baptizing believers in the name of the Father, Son, and Holy Spirit, and teaching them to observe everything Jesus has given us. It is found in Matthew 28:19-20.

Great Disappearance – The Rapture.

Great Tribulation – The last 3.5 years of the Tribulation Period when all hell breaks loose on the Earth. The anti-Christ will show his true colors and will be seen for the evil, wicked, and unholy person that he truly is.

Great White Throne Judgment – The third and final judgment of the world. It happens after the millennial kingdom and before believers enter into eternity. See Revelation 20:11-15.

H –

Heaven, Eternal – What believers inherit for eternity. It is the New Heaven, New Earth, and New Jerusalem. It's permanent.

Heaven, Present – Where Christians go when they die. It's temporary.

Heavenly body – The body you receive at the Rapture. It is spiritual, strong, sinless, and glorious.

Hell – The final destination for Satan, the anti-Christ, the False Prophet, and those who took the mark of the beast (666) during the Tribulation Period. Also called the Lake of Fire.

J –

Judgment Seat of Christ – Takes place in Heaven and is for believers only. Happens immediately after the Rapture. It is not a judgment of sin because believers' sins have been forgiven. It's a judgment of stewardship.

K –

Kingdom of God – The rule of God over the hearts and lives of those who willingly accept Jesus as their Savior. It is both now, in the sense believers submit to the Lordship of Jesus in their lives, and it is future, in the sense that the 1,000 Year Reign of Christ on the Earth is a literal kingdom.

Kingdom kids – Those born during the millennial kingdom. Their parents are those who survive the Tribulation Period by not taking the mark of the beast (666) and are ushered into the millennial kingdom in their earthly bodies.

L –

Lake of Fire – The final and eternal destination of unbelievers. Satan, anti-Christ, False Prophet, those who took the mark of the beast (666), and the armies of the anti-Christ and Satan will be tormented there forever. It is characterized as complete darkness. Also known as Hell.

M –

Mark of the Beast – The mark given to those who pledge their allegiance to the anti-Christ during the Tribulation Period. The mark is "666" and is the number of man.

Marriage Supper of the Lamb – The symbolic marriage and celebration of the raptured church to Jesus.

Messiah – Another name for Jesus.

Mid-Tribulation View – The view that the Rapture takes place in the middle of the 7-year Tribulation Period. Those who believe this view believe the Rapture will take place before the Great Tribulation.

Millennial Kingdom – The 1,000 Year Reign of Christ on the Earth.

N –

Nations Judgment – See Gentile Judgment.

New Earth – A purified version of the original Earth. It is new in the sense that it is purified of all sin, evil, wickedness, and unrighteousness. It is the eternal inheritance of all believers. It will be like the Garden of Eden, only better.

New Heaven – Heaven is always defined as the place where God dwells. In eternity the New Heaven will be down here on the New Earth because God promised He would dwell with men in eternity (Revelation 21:1-3).

New Jerusalem – An actual city that will reside on the New Earth. The holy city is described in Revelation 21:9-27. It is the promised eternal home for Christian believers. Jesus is preparing this city right now (John 14:1-3).

O –

One World Religion – The religion of the Tribulation Period. It is led by the False Prophet and it sees the anti-Christ as its god.

P –

Petra – See Edom.

Post-Tribulation View – The view that the Rapture does not occur until after the Tribulation Period.

Pre-Millennialism – The belief that Jesus' Second Coming will occur before the establishment of the millennial kingdom

Pre-Millennialist – A Christian who believes that Jesus' Second Coming will be before the establishment of the millennial kingdom.

Pre-Tribulation View – The view that the Rapture occurs before the Tribulation Period begins.

R –

Rapture – An event in which God "calls up" all believers, both dead and alive, from the Earth in order to pour out His righteous judgments during the Tribulation Period. It is described in two passages of the Bible. 1 Corinthians 15:50-54 focuses on the instantaneous change of believers, and 1 Thessalonians 4:13-18 focuses on the resurrection of believers. The Rapture and Second Coming are two different events separated by the seven years of the Tribulation Period.

Resurrection – It is the raising of the dead in order to bring them back to life for eternity. For the Christian the resurrection happens at the Rapture when the body is reunited with the soul and spirit.

S –

Seal Judgments – The first set of 7 judgments of God on the Earth during the Tribulation Period. See Revelation 6 and 8:1-5. These judgments are poured out on the Earth over years.

Second Coming – The return of Christ to the Earth to fulfill all remaining prophecies in the Bible. It is spoken of in great detail in Revelation 19:11-16. Jesus will come as a conquering

King with armies following behind Him. He will defeat the anti-Christ and his army at the Battle of Armageddon, and then He will show Himself to Jews at Petra.

Second Death – This is spiritual death, and it is only for unbelievers.

Second Resurrection – This is the resurrection of the dead to the Great White Throne Judgment.

Shekinah Glory of God – The divine presence of God on the Earth. It is evident in the Old Testament as the cloud by day and fire by night for the Israelites in the wilderness. It is evident in the New Testament at Jesus' Transfiguration in Matthew 17:1-13, and at Paul's conversion on the Damascus Road in Acts 9:1-9.

T –

Tribulation Period – The seven-year period in which the wrath of God is poured out on unbelievers of the Earth. It has two primary purposes: To judge all sin, evil, wickedness, and unrighteousness in the world, and to give Israel one last opportunity to accept Jesus as their Messiah. Believers are raptured before the Tribulation Period begins. It will be the worst time in the history of the world.

Trumpet Judgments – The second set of 7 judgments of God on the Earth during the Tribulation Period. See Revelation 8-9, 11:15-19. These judgments are poured out on the Earth over months.

U –

Unholy Trinity – Satan, the anti-Christ, and the False Prophet.

Numbers –

666 – The mark of the beast given to those who pledge their allegiance to the anti-Christ. The mark is forced on the inhabitants of the Earth by the False Prophet. Those who refuse the mark are beheaded.

70th Week – Another name for the Tribulation Period associated with Daniel's Prophecy.

1,000 Year Reign of Christ – The literal physical kingdom that Christ establishes on the Earth after the Tribulation Period and the Gentile Judgment. Jesus will reign as King of the World from Jerusalem, and believers will assist Him as He rules.

GROUP DISCUSSION GUIDE

CHAPTER ONE: THE RAPTURE

MOTIVATION:

- People have been trying to predict Jesus' return since He left. What are your thoughts on the many failed predictions of His return?
- Do you believe the Rapture is fact or fiction? How do you support your belief?

EXAMINATION:

- Discuss the six reasons mentioned in the chapter for a Pre-Tribulation Rapture. Is this convincing enough for you?
- Paul uses the word *"we"* in 1 Thessalonians 4:15 and 17, believing that he would be alive at Christ's return. Discuss what it would be like to be alive at the Rapture?

APPLICATION:

- Believers do not experience the wrath of God. Jesus took upon Himself the punishment for your sin on the cross. Discuss what God's mercy and grace mean to you.
- How does 1 Thessalonians 4:13-18, encourage you today?

CHAPTER TWO: THE NEW HEAVENLY BODY

- Gallop, a Christian research poll, has discovered that 20% of those who call themselves Christians believe in reincarnation. Discuss reincarnation and the resurrection and why they are not compatible with each other.
- Discuss the instantaneous change of the natural body to the spiritual body (*"in the twinkling of an eye"*) and the illustration that Pastor David Dykes gives. What would you say to someone who thinks they will have time to confess, repent, and believe at the Rapture?

EXAMINATION:

- Use Paul's two questions in 1 Corinthians 15:35 and his answer in vv. 36-49, to discuss the characteristics of your new heavenly body.
- Some believe that your resurrected body will be like Jesus' resurrected body, unlimited by time, space, and gravity. As Jesus appeared and disappeared, you will have the same ability in your resurrected body. Discuss your thoughts on this.

APPLICATION:

- What are you most looking forward to in your new heavenly body?
- How will your new heavenly body be like your present earthly body? How will it be different?

MOTIVATION:

- Open your small group by discussing Jesus as your friend and Jesus as your judge.
- Discuss humanity's favorite verse, Matthew 7:1, and humanity's least favorite verse, Matthew 7:5.

EXAMINATION:

- The Judgment Seat of Christ is not about Jesus judging your sin, but about Jesus judging your stewardship. Discuss the difference. Consider Ananias and Sapphira's stewardship in Acts 5:1-11.
- In 1 Corinthians 3:12-15, Paul says fire will reveal what kind of work you have done. Discuss the works of gold, silver, and precious stones with the works of wood, hay, and straw.

APPLICATION:

- What are your thoughts on the idea that someone could be saved but not rewarded? They're in Heaven, but as one escaping as through the fire.
- Review the crowns a believer will receive as a reward at the Judgment Seat of Christ. What could be your crown and why?

CHAPTER FOUR: A MARRIAGE MADE FOR HEAVEN

MOTIVATION:

- If you're married, describe the excitement at your wedding. If you're not married, discuss what you are looking forward to when you get married.
- Now, describe the excitement at your wedding in Heaven. How are the two different?

EXAMINATION:

- What are the meanings in Jesus' parables in Matthew 22:1-14 and Matthew 25:1-13? How are these two parables connected to your marriage to Jesus in Heaven?
- Your marriage in Heaven follows the three stages of a traditional New Testament Jewish marriage. What stage is the church in right now? What stage begins at the Rapture and the Second Coming? Symbolically, what does the Tribulation Period represent in the traditional Jewish wedding?

APPLICATION:

- How do you feel personally about being called the "bride of Christ"?
- What does it mean to you that your earthly marriage is a picture of your heavenly marriage?

MOTIVATION:

- Discuss the "delusion" proposed in the chapter. Do you think this is a valid idea? If not, what do you think the delusion could be?
- One half of the world's population is going to die during the Tribulation Period. Discuss all the possible affects this will have on the world.

EXAMINATION:

- Discuss the three signs leading up to the Tribulation Period in Matthew 24:1-8. Do you think the world is living in this time right now? If so, why? If not, why not?
- People are saved during the Tribulation Period. Discuss the reasons given as proof of their salvation. How is this salvation different from your salvation, which is pre-Rapture and pre-Tribulation?

APPLICATION:

- How does this chapter on the Tribulation Period change the way you will live your life today, and in the future?
- Does this change the way you will witness to the lost today? If so, how?

CHAPTER SIX: THE SECOND COMING OF CHRIST

MOTIVATION:

- Revelation 19:11 calls Jesus Faithful and True. In the world today, faith and truth are dying. Discuss the corruption in governments, courtrooms, and boardrooms. How will this change when Jesus returns?
- The Bible says, *"Every eye will see Him..."* How do you think the whole world will see Jesus' return? Do you think present technology and maybe even new technology will be used?

EXAMINATION:

- Read Matthew 24:29-31 and Revelation 16:12-21, and discuss the signs leading up to Christ's return.
- A purpose of the Second Coming is for Jesus to reveal Himself to the Jews who have escaped to Petra. There is great mourning and rejoicing when they see Him. Why?

APPLICATION:

- How does the certainty of Jesus' Second Coming impact your life today?
- What are you personally looking forward to most when you return with Jesus at His Second Coming?

CHAPTER SEVEN: THE MILLENNIAL REIGN OF CHRIST ON THE EARTH

MOTIVATION:

- Discuss the importance of Jesus' millennial reign on the Earth, and why it is important that the world see Him as "KING OF KINGS and LORD OF LORDS."
- The characteristics of peace, justice, and truth will be taught to everyone during the millennial kingdom. How will Jesus achieve this, and why can't the world achieve this today?

EXAMINATION:

- Discuss the survivors of the Tribulation Period inheriting the millennial kingdom in their natural, physical bodies with the ability to procreate for 1,000 years.
- Some believe there is no death during the millennial kingdom. If Adam, Seth, Enosh, Noah, and Methuselah can live to be over 900 years old, then longevity of life will return. What are your thoughts?

APPLICATION:

- Do you think it's possible that God could use the actual people of the Bible to teach their personal experiences recorded in the Bible to the kingdom kids? If you had that experience today, how would it change your faith?
- You will be assisting Jesus as He reigns on the Earth for 1,000 years. What job do you think you will have in the kingdom, and do you think it will be related to your present spiritual gift?

CHAPTER EIGHT: SATAN'S LAST STAND

MOTIVATION:

- Discuss Satan as an "expert at observational intelligence" when he attacks you.
- Discuss the external attacks and the internal attacks of Satan. Using Job as an example, how did Satan attack him externally and internally?

EXAMINATION:

- Isaiah 14:3-21 describes the King of Babylon, and Ezekiel 28:11-19 describes the King of Tyre. Do you agree or disagree, that these two passages are representative of Satan? Why or why not?
- Satan is released at the end of the millennial kingdom. Discuss reasons given in the chapter as to why God releases him.

APPLICATION:

- Satan uses "fiery darts" to tempt you. What "fiery darts" does Satan use against you today?
- How can you use the "armor of God" (Ephesians 6:10-18), to combat Satan's attacks against you?

CHAPTER NINE: THE GREAT WHITE THRONE JUDGMENT

MOTIVATION:

- If you have ever been a part of the justice system, as a witness, jurist, or defendant/plaintiff, discuss your experience.
- How has the world taken the reality and severity out of Hell? Why has the world done this?

EXAMINATION:

- Every person ever born will be at the Great White Throne Judgment, but Christians will not be judged; they will be spectators and witnesses. Do you agree or disagree? Why or why not?
- Discuss the first and second death, along with the first and second resurrection as mentioned in the chapter.

APPLICATION:

- Discuss the reality of the Lake of Fire (Hell)— complete loneliness and darkness and eternal torment. How does this motivate you to witness to the unsaved around you today?
- What would you say to a person who believes Hell is just another place to go after death and makes jokes about going there?

MOTIVATION:

- Before the group session, read Revelation 21-22 and write down everything about eternity that you see. Use this list in your discussion with the group.
- Discuss the difference between present Heaven and eternal Heaven.

EXAMINATION:

- Discuss what you think eternal Heaven will be like. Will we have jobs in Heaven? Will we sleep in Heaven? Will our pets be in Heaven? How will we worship in Heaven? Will we entertain people in our heavenly homes? How will we interact with God in Heaven?
- Read Revelation 21:24. Who do you believe the nations and kings of the New Earth are?

APPLICATION:

- Imagine the beauty of the New Jerusalem. Jesus created the world in six days, and He has been gone 2,000 years creating a home for us (John 14:1-3), so the New Jerusalem must be better in every way compared to the present Earth. What are you most looking forward to leaving behind on Earth when you arrive in eternity? What are you most looking forward to doing when you get to eternity?
- What are you doing today to ensure your final reservation for your final destination is secure?

ABC'S OF SALVATION

God never intended salvation to be difficult. His plan of salvation is simple enough for you to understand. In fact, it's as easy as ABC.

Admit

Admit that you are a sinner. The Bible says that everyone has a problem with sin, from the richest to the poorest, from the youngest to the oldest.

> **Romans 3:23:** *For all have sinned, and fall short of the glory of God.*

> **Romans 6:23:** *For the wages of sin is death, but the gift of God is eternal life through Christ Jesus our Lord.*

Believe

Believe that Jesus Christ is the Son of God and that He died on the cross to forgive you of all your sins. He is the only way to salvation and the only way to eternity in Heaven. You have done nothing to deserve God's salvation; He simply gives it to you because He loves you.

John 3:16: For God so loved the world in this way: He gave his One and Only Son, so that everyone who believes in Him will not perish, but have eternal life.

John 14:6: Jesus told him, "I am the way and the truth and the life. No one comes to the Father except through Me."

Confess

Confess your sins and commit your life to Jesus Christ.

1 John 1:9: If we confess our sins, he is faithful and righteous to forgive us our sins and cleanse us all unrighteousness.

Romans 10:9-10: If you confess with your mouth, "Jesus is Lord," and believe in your heart that God raised Him from the dead, you will be saved. With the heart one believes, resulting in righteousness, and with the mouth one confesses, resulting in salvation.

Pray

Lord Jesus, I know I'm a sinner. But I believe You died on the cross to forgive me of my sins. I believe You were raised from the dead on the third day, and now You are in Heaven preparing an eternal home for me. I accept You as my Savior, my Lord, and my Friend. Thank You for giving me the free gift of eternal life. I love You!

Contact Information

For information about The Second Coming of Jesus please visit: www.noliverbooks.com.

ENDNOTES

Chapter 1: The Rapture

1   Rick Warren, *The Purpose Driven Life*, (Zondervan, Grand Rapids, MI., 2002), 50.
2   sermonillustrations.com/a-z/r/rapture.htm, *Today In The Word*, (April 28, 1993).
3   J. Dwight Pentecost, *Things To Come, A Study In Biblical Eschatology*, (Zondervan, Grand Rapids, MI., 1958), 210.
4   Rick Warren, *The Purpose-Driven Life*, (Zondervan, Grand Rapids, MI., 2002), 33-34.
5   Robert Russell, *Resurrection Promises*, (sermon, Southeast Christian Church, Louisville, KY).
6   sermonillustrations.com/a-z/r/rapture.htm, Our Daily Bread.

Chapter 2: The New Heavenly Body

7   Hank Hanegraaf, *Resurrection*, (Thomas Nelson, Nashville, TN., 2000), 70.
8   Randy Alcorn, *Heaven*, (Tyndale, Carol Stream, Ill., 2004), quote, R.A. Torrey, 112.
9   David O. Dykes, Are You Ready For The Rapture?, (sermon preached Green Acres Baptist Church, Tyler, TX, October 9, 2014), sermon central.com
10 Benjamin, Franklin, *The Body of Benjamin Franklin*, (quote from goodreads.com).
11 Randy Alcorn, *Heaven*, (Tyndale, Carol Stream, Ill., 2004), 283.
12 Joni Eareckson Tada, *Heaven: Your Real Home*, (Zondervan, Grand Rapid, MI., 1985), 39.

Chapter 3: The Judgment Seat of Christ

13   Alexander Maclaren, *When I Stand At The Judgment Seat*, https://bible.org./illustration/ when-i-stand-judgment-seat.
14   James Denney, quote from sermonillustrations.com/a-z/j/judgment -seat-of-christ.

Chapter 4: A Marriage Made for Heaven

15   Charles H. Spurgeon, quote from azquotes.com/quote.

Chapter 5: The Tribulation Period

16   Sir Robert Anderson, *The Coming Prince*, (Kregel Classics, 1957), xii-xiii.

Chapter 6: The Second Coming of Christ

17   Tim LaHaye, quote from christianquotes.info.

Chapter 7: The Millennial Reign of Christ on the Earth

18   Billy Graham, Storm Warning, (Word Publishing, Dallas, TX., 1992), 297-298.

Chapter 8: Satan's Last Stand

19   Wikipedia, The Free Encyclopedia, George Armstrong Custer, Battle of Little Big Horn.
20   Charles Stanley, When The Enemy Strikes, (Thomas Nelson, Inc., Nashville, TN., 2004), 35.
21   Walter Scott, *Exposition of the Revelation of Jesus Christ*, (London: Pickering an Inglis, n.d.), 407.
22   David Jeremiah, *Escape the Coming Night*, (W Publishing, Nashville, TN., 2018), 245.

Chapter 9: The Great White Throne Judgment

23 The Baptist Hymnal, *When We All Get To Heaven*, (Convention Press, Nashville, TN., 1991), 514.
24 Azquotes.com/quote/139122

Chapter 10: Eternity In Heaven

25 Randy Alcorn, *Heaven* (Tyndale, Carol Stream, Ill., 2004), 132.
26 Anthony Hoekema, *Heaven: Not Just An Eternal Day Off*, (Christianity Today, June 6, 2003).